# From Sin
## to
# Wholeness

# From Sin
## to
# Wholeness

*By*

BRIAN W. GRANT

THE WESTMINSTER PRESS
*Philadelphia*

BOOK DESIGN BY DOROTHY ALDEN SMITH


*First edition*

Published by The Westminster Press®
Philadelphia, Pennsylvania

PRINTED IN THE UNITED STATES OF AMERICA
9 8 7 6 5 4 3 2 1

**Library of Congress Cataloging in Publication Data**

Grant, Brian W., 1939–
    From sin to wholeness.

    Includes bibliographical references.
    1. Deadly sins. 2. Pastoral psychology.
3. Christian life—Disciples authors. I. Title
BV4626.G73        241'.3        81–16122
ISBN 0–664–24399–1                    AACR2

# Contents

# PART I

# *Of Sin and Sinning*

---

# 1. Introduction

Sin has become an acceptable topic in the mainline church again. The psychiatrist Karl Menninger insisted several years ago in *Whatever Became of Sin?* (Hawthorn Books, 1973) that we not write off all unpleasant behavior as maladjustment or reduce evil to a legal problem by calling it crime. Don Browning invited the church to return to a discussion of what is and isn't moral in *The Moral Context of Pastoral Care* (Westminster Press, 1976). Both recognized that providing guidance for life is an important function of the church, and that our existing understanding of what is right and what is wrong is seriously out of date in many instances.

The church's interest in sin stems from the certainty that people can ruin their own lives and the lives of others by carrying out actions and setting up situations that do violence to everyone's human possibilities. At various times in history the church has been certain what those actions and situations are, and has spoken clearly to encourage people to exclude them from their lives. That clarity has undoubtedly been effective in warning millions against dangers that could have destroyed them.

Unfortunately clarity has a way of lasting longer than the situations in which it makes sense; and once the church has said that something is wrong it has always been difficult to change that belief when circumstances changed. As a result, we have two well-demarcated positions within the church today. In one camp are those who hold that if the church has ever said something was wrong, it is still wrong. In the other camp are those who claim that many things we once said were wrong are not wrong, or at least not always wrong. That leaves unanswered the question of whether there is any way to decide what, if anything, is wrong today.

On the one hand, such uncertainty appears ludicrous, when you see the amount of misery humanity creates for itself every day. But on the other hand it is easily understandable, because so many Christians who are sure about what is right and what is wrong are sure in such a reason-defying way and about so many questionable or trivial realities that they make a very easy target. So the church needs believable spokespersons who are willing to call specific acts sinful.

This book is an effort to meet that need. It attempts to look at particular things people do, and to decide which fit and which do not fit the oldest set of criteria for sin that the church has. It attempts to do so in a way that takes seriously how personalities are formed. It assumes that some things we have always thought were sinful probably were and still are, but that many we once thought were sinful no longer fit the description. It is clear that sin destroys life. It is also clear that the standard Christian strategy for dealing with that reality is not working well, and that we need a new one. This book will attempt to offer a new strategy.

## How We Learn About Sin and About Life

Most of us first learned how to feel good in life by following rules, by doing what someone else said we should. We learned that our mother would smile when we ate our cereal, drank our milk, and brushed our teeth. We learned that she would frown, or speak harshly, or even hit us, when we wet our pants, took our little brother's toy, or repeated the interesting words the big kids down the block were using.

Our first learnings about religion followed the same pattern. We learned the Ten Commandments, and the interpretations of them that our Sunday school teachers, and later our pastors, took most seriously. We were taught not to swear, steal, lie, or touch ourselves in the wrong places. We understood that by paying attention to those rules we would become good little boys and girls, that Jesus would love us, and that heaven would be our reward. It probably isn't accidental that by following those rules we also maintained a relatively calm and orderly existence for our parents and for any institution that had to deal with us extensively.

By the time we reached adolescence we had discovered that, though the comforts and securities gained by following the rules were real, other and greater rewards could often be had by breaking them. As we struggled toward independent adulthood, our peers came to see our willingness to bear the punishment for refusing to go along as a mark of courage, maturity, and acceptability. We didn't notice then that it is just as slavish to break every rule as to obey every rule, and to accept the tyranny of our adolescent society as to accept that of our parents.

Some of us, of course, never reached that point; and others have never passed it. The former continue in their thirties or forties to feel like children waiting for an adolescence; and the latter feel like those who are forever seventeen, mistaking their chronic rebellion for the independence of adulthood.

We carry enough of our parents inside our heads that we are often tempted to label the second group sinners and the first group Christians. Popular religion helps us believe in those labels, as do the generally pious utterances of police chiefs, school principals, and various political figures advocating law and order. Though the church's theology does go much deeper on these points, and its psychology could, much of its public rhetoric can be read as a demand for untroubling, rule-following behavior.

"Avoid sin" has so often appeared to be our watchword that probably half the religious people and three quarters of everyone else would see it as the central message of Christianity. Over the centuries that misinterpretation was strengthened by the medieval church through its religious use of the ancient list of seven capital (later reinterpreted to "deadly") sins, and is maintained by the continuing use of this checklist in today's Catholic penitential practice. We Protestants have contributed mightily with our endorsement as Christian of the life of anyone who omits at least three of the following dangers: alcohol, tobacco, movies, dancing, cards, trying to look attractive, or responding to those who do.

## SIN IS REAL, DESPITE US

The tragedy of this situation is that it invites people to poke fun at the trivialization of a life-and-death concern. We tend to forget that there are real sins, acts that truly damage self and others, and that such acts are offensive to God and to Christian conscience.

History tells us that the classic list of seven sins has roots in pre-Christian times. The original compilers of lists of sins were grappling with an actual and immense problem. They were trying to identify those human actions which damage life, so that such actions could more readily be avoided and life could more often be good. No matter how their product has been misused, their aim was not primarily to proclaim themselves holier than others. They were seeking a real quarry, one that needed then and needs now to be identified and exposed.

What is the quarry? And what are the dangers if it is allowed to run free?

I define "sin" as whatever we do or are that destroys, for ourselves or another, the reality or possibility of life lived in communion with God, whether we acknowledge that fact or not. One can substitute many words for "destroys"— including "delays," "diminishes," "obstructs," or "dilutes." All identify acts that interfere with a person's state of peace with one's neighbor and oneself, with the natural world and its Creator. Since I subscribe to the belief that the human person is happiest when that peace is finally achieved, I would hold that any sin against God also produces dislocation and unhappiness in the human realm for at least the sinner, and often for many others as well.

The magnitude of the danger varies widely and can be looked at from a number of positions. From the perspective of a citizen of the world community, I see sin's ability to foul the environment, to create cities where it's not safe to walk the streets at night, to produce in everyone the constant fear of war and genocide, and to build a widening gap between those rich in worldly power and those without it. It is clear that these effects of sin may destroy all human beings and the chance for there to ever be any more. Even if that does not happen, it is clear that we are paying now through environmentally created illnesses, racial antagonisms, and the staggering though necessary costs of national defense. From another perspective, that of a pastoral psychotherapist, I see the sins of the parents visited upon the sons and daughters to the third and subsequent generations in the form of the inability to love, the fear of ever believing in one's own decisions, the refusal to trust anyone, and the overarching belief that life is a troublesome series of events from which no joy can be expected. The ultimate tragedy, from this perspective, is the death of a person who never discovered that life could be joyous, that the world God created has in it everything needed for human fulfillment—that "it works," as George Burns aptly stated in the film *Oh, God.* Too many believing Christians go to their graves without discovering that life can be fulfilled, and that although evil can rule over good, it does not have to!

## How It Happens

How did we get into such a mess? In the absence of necessity, and in the face of such terrible penalties, how have we allowed sin such power that it seems able to crush out the signs of goodness and grace in the lives of so many? To begin answering that question we need to take a brief look at human development. Each one of us is born into an incredibly complex set of relationships with other persons, physical circumstances, and the histories thereof. We are born with no knowledge of what produces human happiness, except the knowledge given to us first by our parents, which in most cases is only a very slight modification of what was given to them by their parents, and to them by theirs. Solutions to human problems that actually did work at one point in geography and history tend to become institutionalized and remain binding when the people who hold them move to other parts of the world and come into contact with new technologies or new limitations. So we each have our set of solutions, congealed into rules. A rule such as "Don't play in the street" is very useful and life-saving in outer-city or inner-suburban neighborhoods in the United States in the 1980s. But the same rule would be meaningless in an inner-city slum where there is no place else to play, or in a fashionable cul-de-sac in the outer suburbs where it is impossible to drive more than ten miles an hour. And who knows what may become of rules like that if there is a severe shortage of fuel for automobiles? But for my children, where I live now, it is an important and life-saving rule, one that I recognize as such partly because it was a good rule for me at a certain point in my own childhood.

Other rules are not so fruitful. My childhood was greatly

influenced by a grandmother whose own childhood had been only a few years behind the movement of the frontier through Kansas and Oklahoma. She had learned thoroughly the maxim that "idle hands are the devil's tools" at a time and place in which physical survival depended on getting the maximum possible production of goods out of every member of every household all the time. Inactivity was seen as the enemy of production, and therefore of life. She carefully taught my father, who well taught me (with her periodically looking over his shoulder). Coming into young adulthood in the somewhat more comfortable mid-1960s, it took me several years of expensive and painful psychotherapy to be able to stop producing long enough to have a chance to develop relationships, to learn to love, and to give something other than products to those I cared about. What had been a good rule in 1900 in rural Kansas was a very destructive rule a half century later in an urban environment.

But I learned, as did millions of my contemporaries, not to play in the street and to work very hard most of the time. Following those rules kept me alive, but they did not do much of a job of keeping me at peace with my neighbors, myself, and the physical world and its Creator. This is the condition of many of us who learn the rules and for the most part follow them, at least up to a certain age. Having followed them, we discover—usually between the ages of five and twenty-five—that a life consisting primarily of following this or any other set of rules simply will not make us happy, will not bring us peace with those elements of self and world with which we must deal. In my experience, many of the clients who come for counseling do so precisely because they realize, in their twenties and thirties, that they have followed the rules their parents set down for them, the rules they thought God had originated and passed down through the church, and that the promised rewards for following them simply are not forthcoming. They become disillusioned, enraged, or depressed, and they come to us looking for a solution to a problem produced by always choosing the supposedly right solutions.

Those of us who get beyond the psychological age of ten have figured that out. We discover that some of the things we were taught we must do to live decent lives were just plain wrong. We become angry, resentful, and often vengeful. Typically we rebel. We select a few of the rules that we especially dislike and we make it our new central intention to disobey them, as it once was to follow them. We drink, we gamble, we have sex with people we're not married to, we lie to cover our tracks, and we lash out against institutions our parents valued or we join those they rejected. Typically the world rises up and denounces us as dangerous people, subversive influences, immoral wastrels, or what have you—and we rejoice for having gotten its attention.

This rebellion itself is not the sin, though many would say that it is. Most often rebellion is a desperate attempt to get what can be had from life, a mandatory attempt if the individual is ever to achieve an adult sense of mastery over the world. Most of us act like idiots for a couple of years—or maybe eight or ten years—and then look around and notice that we have won the freedom we were seeking to win, and that we don't like the destruction we are currently leaving in our wake. We decide to keep the freedom and some of the ways we used to get it, but gradually begin modifying our lives into more responsible and promising paths. If we do this well, there is a good chance that by the time we reach thirty we will sense ourselves as being in charge of our own lives and at peace with the world and our neighbors.

When that happens, we have escaped our slavery to the sins of our parents and have settled into a world conditioned by both their sins and their achievements, a world that is free for the molding we offer it with our own hands.

## When It Happens

In the process of this pilgrimage, we are always vulnerable to sins and sinning—but we can identify the points of greatest vulnerability to specific sins. Each of those points has its own specialized sins, and the effect of each is different. First there are the sins of a falsely extended childhood, which fall under the classical banners of sloth and gluttony. Sloth marks the childhood that can be found in people— from their teens to their eighties—who have decided it is too dangerous and too evil to ever enter into their own "rebellious adolescence," and who instead have decided to accept the world as their parents gave it to them. This acceptance denies them the possibility of having any independent judgment or making any contribution to the world, and thereby of being a responsible adult in it. It is often a depressed and despairing acceptance, rather than a happy one, because the world is changing so rapidly that almost any acceptance of it on anyone's parents' terms will leave a person in important ways ill equipped to deal with what is present. Those who are thus ill equipped will be unsuccessful and dissatisfied, but, lacking the courage to forfeit their parents' good favor (and that of a world full of their parents' real and imagined allies), they will despairingly remain static believers in the ultimate wrongness of taking independent—and sometimes unacceptable—action. Such sloth often leads to illness, depression, lives felt to be empty and ended with suicide. But even without such dramatic results it saps the sufferers of their creativity and denies the world their potential contribution.

While sloth is the sin that obstructs our laying hold of life and giving ourselves to it, gluttony is our childlike way of trying to take back from it more than we have produced. It is the attempt to deny our sloth by fearfully overrewarding ourselves. If we are not producing, we have all the more time and feel all the more need to consume, as we did when we were children. We take the view that the world is there for our consumption. We suck at the breast of mother earth, unwilling to release her and go about our business, because we fear that we will never be able to get her back.

Then there are the sins of misplaced adolescence. These have anger and lust at their root, and work themselves out —as do the sins of childhood—through the involvement of all the others. In the sins of extended adolescence, the sinner has achieved the power to make his or her own life decisions. But, while achieving this power, one has become so addicted to the heady triumph of nonsubmission that one does not appropriately relinquish it in time, but carries on, not noticing the absence of continuing opposition. This particular set of sins is fostered by a style of parenting that denies children the right to make decisions about their lives, and that carries this denial well past the age of accountability. If the "parentee" ever escapes childhood, a lasting rebellion is practically guaranteed.

If the child's autonomy has been systematically abused by parents and those parents claim a valuable set of beliefs, then a two-pronged danger is established: (1) It will feel exhilarating and justified for the maturing child to throw off the oppression of the rule-believer. (2) It will never feel quite safe for this person to accept those original parental beliefs, because he or she will be convinced that such a giving in will bring with it the indignities that go with losing control of one's life. If you carry around that much fear and anger, the suggestion that you doubt that you can still be so easily overpowered may sound like the enemy's first move in the attempt to reestablish control over you. Since that enemy's words can come in such subtle ways, our extended adolescent feels justified in making fearful and angry response to a similar wide range of possibilities. In keeping the proverbial nose of the camel well away from the tent, one often prevents oneself from finding out that it was really a harmless kitten. It should come as no surprise that the kitten is often killed in the process.

Extended adolescents, thus protected by the anger that cuts off any examination of their behavior, will often continue all their lives in the form of the rebellion that first won their apparent freedom. You will find people in their forties and fifties cynically rejecting every effort of governmental or private structures to modify the world's pain, laughing at the efforts of churches or service clubs, and seriously damaging their own chances for an enjoyable life by drinking themselves into one crisis after another or touching off endless rounds of marital warfare with multiple and unneeded flirtations.

But it is the sins of mature adulthood that are the hardest to understand, control, or even clearly identify. That is so partly because mature adulthood itself is a rare achievement, but even those who understand that still have a difficult problem on their hands. These are people who wield the greatest power, so their sins have the widest range of destructive potential. They are persons whose slavery to childish and adolescent patterns is effectively broken, so their sins are the hardest to predict and thereby to defend against. Because theirs are the sins of psychologically healthier people, they are sins for which there are no established patterns of cure.

If there are any sins for which individuals are solely and singularly responsible, they are the sins of mature adulthood. These are not the repetitive patterns that one learned in collusion with one's parents, or discovered as an effective way of turning the tables on them. Adult sins often arise from the independent, nonpatterned exercise of free will, standing out in contrast to an apparently well ordered and useful life.

The sins of adulthood point to a dilemma for those who see sin as the breaking of a rule. Many adult sins are acts of collusion with large numbers of other adults in the production and perpetuation of social evils—racial injustice, eco-

nomic exploitation, intentional ignorance, etc. These often
appear to be acts that no one is individually responsible for,
but that grind on with inexorable effects precisely because
there is no point at which they can be challenged. They are
often the result of one group following a set of rules that
are a source of destruction to others who live among them.
Each person has responsibility for his or her own action in
the perpetuation and establishment of such a sin—and we
often bear the effects of that responsibility in our own unhappiness—but it is difficult to determine that any one person should be blamed and/or punished for it. The more
psychotherapists learn about the systems in which human
beings function, the less it is possible to tell an individual
that he or she is to blame for anything.

That brings us finally to the ancient list itself: the seven
deadly sins. This list of sins—pride, avarice, sloth, lust, gluttony, envy, and anger—was the result of a thousand years
of medieval effort to decide on the most damaging human
acts. These sins were originally termed the capital sins,
because it was believed that all sinful acts sprang from some
combination of them. They were not originally thought of
as deadly (meaning that the person would go to hell for
certain if these sins were committed and not repented), but
were instead seen as the root sins from which all others
grew.[1]

They fit especially well into the Roman Catholic process
of individual confession as it developed at the end of the
ancient world, and spawned the Protestant habit of looking
to individual behavior for the sources of things most abhor-
rent to God and destructive to human life. It was also convenient that the priest could designate a particular penance
for a particular sin, and it later was convenient for Protestant preachers to assure their hearers that if they avoided
these or other specific vices, their eternal salvation was assured.

When we govern our lives by the attempt to avoid the sins

on this list or any other, we face a very powerful question: Can sin be avoided by the attempt to avoid sin? Is this possible, given our unknowing collective participation in evil, given the fact that historical relativity makes an act sinful in one context and not another, and given our own inability to know our motives truly at all times? Can we, by choosing, avoid falling into the snares of whatever offense against God we have come to believe is the most dangerous? And if we have such monumental questions about our own behavior, how can we judge the actions of others?

That brings me to the overall point and plan for this book. The point, simply, is that by structuring our lives around the attempt to avoid sin we tend to produce more sin rather than less. To show how that is so, I will discuss each entry on the famous list. I will try to show what good aim is being sought in the behavior that is distorted into the sin in question. I will attempt to define where the normal and creative ends and where the sin begins. I will discuss the actual dangers to self and others of continued indulgence in the sin. I will describe the typical ways this particular sin develops in the life of the person. I will show how the time-honored attempts to avoid this sin have been made, and what are their advantages and disadvantages. I will point out the social participation in both the sin and the way in which we avoid it. And I will attempt to show how the vigorous attempt to gain the good end originally sought by the behavior in question is more productive for human life than the attempt to simply avoid the sin, even though there are pitfalls along that more productive path as well. I think we will find that there are clear implications in this discussion for all human life, so that we will finish knowing more about ourselves and not just about our sin.

# PART II

# The Sins of Misplaced Childhood

## 2. Sloth—Apathy

When we were very young, rest was our natural state. As infants we slept twenty hours a day, and the management of the world was left to others while we tended to the business of taking nourishment and awaiting the growth of our bodies. In the normal course of things, as we grow and become more capable we take more and more of the world under our management and become increasingly responsible for the fulfillment of our own lives. If we are skilled, courageous, and lucky, there will come a time, perhaps in our twenties or thirties, when we can honestly say that we are responsible for the satisfactions and dissatisfactions of our own lives. We know that we have achieved that when we have stopped blaming others for what they have done to us, stopped placing our hopes in their changing so we can be happy, and started changing the world ourselves and building on the foundations God has put here for us to make life rich and full.

But for all of us there remains some false residue of what was true in childhood—the belief that there is really nothing we can do to bring the world closer to the way we want it. For some of us that becomes the central idea of life, which subsequently becomes focused in the indirect and manipulative attempt to get somebody else to make things better for us—since we believe that neither God nor we ourselves can do it.

To the extent that we mire ourselves in the effects of this sin of sloth, it is likely that we learned as children that our efforts would not affect the world. For some children, the root of this belief lies in their parents' subtle discouraging of every independent act, and the subsequently great rewards that those same parents bestow for the children's modeling themselves almost completely around what the parents appear to want them to be. When that experience is repeated day after day for thousands of times, it feels less and less important (and less possible) to answer the questions, "What do I want?" "What do I like?" and "What will I do?" than to pay attention to "What does she want?" "What does he like?" and "What do they want me to do?"

The reason this sin is placed in childhood is that this sort of temptation for the growing infant begins almost immediately. In any family there is a mixture of enthusiasm and dismay when a very young child begins to do things on its own, whether those things are the excitement-producing kind, like talking or walking, or the annoying kind, like breaking things and screaming in the middle of the night. The enthusiasm comes from obvious sources, the parents' satisfaction that their child is making the appropriate strides toward maturity. The dismay is less obvious, except for the occasions when the child is doing inconvenient things; but in some families, where parents are especially concerned about doing the right things (the things *their* parents have told them are right), it is difficult for the child to gain rewards by doing anything other than what the parents have already prescribed. Independent action in these families is not rewarded, even if it appears helpful or growthful to outsiders. A child growing up in such a family begins to notice that the only behavior that brings a smile to mother's face or gets a word of praise from dad is doing something the child has already been told to do. The behavior won't be punished if it is original with the child, it just won't be noticed. Because children need the reinforcement that comes from pleasing parents, more and more they will expect that the only good feelings come, not from noticing what they want to do and doing it, but from getting someone else to tell them what to do and then doing that. To behave otherwise in such a home is to be constantly lonely, and increasingly to see your parents as disappointed in you and preferring someone else. Children will not choose to continue in that situation if they are aware of an alternative, so they will increasingly choose to paralyze their own self-initiation and rely more and more on the slothful option of waiting for the other to produce the beginning of all behavior.

To the extent that initiative has been thoroughly drilled out of such children, they are more and more the slaves of a set of images and wishes that fit another person in another place. With their natural perceptions and impulses turned off in favor of those they are attempting to pick up from the other, their responses will inevitably lack the precision and spontaneity shown by persons in tune with self and the world. When you attempt to deal with the world from that basis, you consistently miss the mark. Failure becomes a regular, expectable occurrence, reinforcing the belief that if you simply will wait for someone else to tell you, the chances of success are far greater. Such studied and consistent passivity inevitably breeds discontent; not the divine discontent that leads to creative action, but the discouraged depression that schools hopelessness, inaction, and withdrawal from the world.

This is the heart of the sin of *acedia* or *accidie*, which is the Greek word in the original lists. Most translators have equated it with "sloth" in English, but the Greek is more properly rendered "uncaring." Commentators have also labeled it dejection, despair, boredom, gloom, and sluggishness, though we will say "sloth" hereafter to avoid confusion. It leads to a multitude of evils. It produces the slowness of heart that paralyzes response in the face of pain, anesthetizing us, blocking our ability to intervene in calamities ranging from the Holocaust to the loneliness of one's neighbor. It produces the drag on creativity and productivity that leaves us feeling a pointlessness about searching our minds or putting out the extra effort to do this last piece of work promptly and well. It is involved in the gradual decline of American economic productivity and the increasing expectation that no one really has the right to insist on work of high quality in any area of life. It promotes a general gloom, a belief that our best efforts will still not be good enough to solve the problems, so—what the hell—we may as well do just enough to get by. Where this spiral of sullen demandingness, inaction, and the expectation that it's up to somebody else will lead, none of us can exactly predict, but I have the uneasy feeling that we may soon find out, and that we will not like the finding.

At the individual level, the results are more certain and no less unpleasant. Here we have the person, irony of ironies, who has become convinced that what he or she would spontaneously do would be the wrong thing, would be either a sin in the eyes of someone more important or simply not of sufficient magnitude to matter. So independent activity, the following of the wishes that energize and empower us all, is gradually abandoned. Since only those things which someone else wants are safe to do, and one has gradually lost touch with even what it is that one does want oneself, it is hard to mobilize the energy to do anything at all. The only permissible actions serve someone else's wishes, not one's own; it is no wonder they are boring.

Into this boredom creeps a gradual and deepening sadness. It reaches the proportions that John of Damascus called "an oppressive grief." In this position one is disgusted with oneself and at the same time senses a hopelessness about even discovering what one would ask the other to do to make things better. At the extremity of this condition no help is expected from the outside, as one has lost the belief that anything can be done. The world, the self, and one's neighbor all appear equally to be a source of no good thing.

It is into this situation that all manner of self-destruction comes, from suicide to the proliferation of pseudo activity generated to keep the mind away from the hopelessness about doing anything real. A number of socially problematic pastimes can be tried to banish the awareness, on this oldest route of human misery—with alcohol, drugs, and the other anesthetics of promiscuous sex and gratuitous violence heading the list. Whenever we see a person moving back and forth from boredom to outrageous behavior we should expect to find sloth at its base.

This is the sin of the one-talent man, in the parable of the talents, and of the foolish virgins, in the parable of the wise and foolish virgins. In both cases that which should have been done was left undone, and the rewards God makes available for life were missed. It is not mere laziness that the Gospels chronicle here, but a basically fearful stance toward the world on the one hand and a haphazard inattention to the necessities of life on the other. Both sets of losers suffer from a false view of the world and of Him who brings its rewards, in both cases a view that does not allow proper dignity and necessity to the effort of this particular human being. As a result, they bear the punishment for what William May identifies as the only sin for which payment is not deferred.[2]

Some have seen a way to avoid the temptation to sloth by constantly driving themselves to produce more than they really want to, in the belief that if they ever let themselves relax, they would accomplish nothing at all, and thus would fall under a terrible judgment. These people can be very productive in the fashion in which slaves are productive. A woman I knew used to begin vigorously cleaning the house every time she felt bad. The aunt who had raised her had really only liked her when she was doing household duties, so, even as an adult, whenever she felt unliked she would regularly dust three tables and empty all the wastebaskets. This frenetic cleaning of a house that was already clean would probably have scored points with the aunt in question, but she was never around to see it. So this woman had one of the most orderly houses in the county, but rarely got around to asking why she had no friends.

Billy Graham is one of the foremost advocates of countering spiritual slothfulness with physical activity—which amounts to a cover-up, not a cure, of this sin. In a sermon on slothfulness, he wrote that it extends into many areas, such as "being slothful about your personal cleanliness which is close to godliness; being slothful about the smile that should be upon the face of every Christian at all times, no matter what the circumstances . . ."[3] Other writers have warned of the dangers of time spent merely doing nothing, and have urged our constant attention to the Pauline injunction to "pray without ceasing." Such prescriptions come from the belief that if people were left to their own devices, they would do nothing, because the natural state of the organism is to do nothing. But that is false. The natural state of the organism is an alternation between vigorous activity and rest, with various stages of activity in between. Activity that seeks a goal a person wants is enjoyable, and will be chosen for that reason. It is only activity imposed from outside which is avoided as unpleasant, and that avoidance is based on a trustworthy natural instinct.

The fatal error in Graham's well-intended advice is the failure to see that activity undertaken only for the sake of avoiding slothfulness deepens the despairing belief that I can get no satisfaction out of my purposeful acts. I will work hard so that it appears to others and myself that I am doing something (or at least not nothing), but we both know down deep that my action comes from my acceptance of the world exactly on the terms that have been dictated to me. Such action is not my own, but really belongs to and will gratify only the person who dictated the terms. It is both symptomatic of and productive of sloth, for it stems from the willingness to be an inert object, manipulated into movement by the will of another. Even the gratification of the other will be imperfect—unless that person gets kicks from ordering people around—because the slothful and automaton-like quality of the performance will produce results of the poorest quality.

This idolatry of works freezes life on a horizontal plane and convinces us that all merit and virtue are to be had by following directions and getting out the product. The only counter to this slothful zeal is to move to levels of more natural though less apparent activity, and to find the rewards in a way that allows us to relativize what comes from following orders. None of those activities can be done for another person, so each yields what it gives us as uniquely our own. Further, each comes to us from a level of life different from work, and lets us see work more clearly in comparison to activities that provide other sorts of rewards.

Nevertheless, this sort of slavery to the internalized other has been the basis for much of the character formation of persons in the Christian world since the industrial revolution. It has been assumed that to work is always good, to goof off is always bad, and that joy awaits him (and increasingly her) who labors hardest and accumulates most. In some circles that has even been extended to the point where the same speakers proclaim that to follow all the rules is always right, to demand a hearing for one's own thinking is always wrong, and the greatest rewards will go to those who make the fewest waves. It is true that these are very safe ways to live as the world counts safety, but they are very likely to lead to the loss of one's own freedom to be a co-creator of the world with God and one's fellows. Furthermore, as every successful capitalist knows, if he or she had lived that way, it wouldn't have been possible to make a nickel; and if everybody lived that way, we'd all still be living off gathered nuts and berries and be dying of old age at twenty-five.

But we will still be sold the belief—if we will buy—that salvation can be had by works, and that the necessary works are prescribed by others and not originated within ourselves. We are to do exactly what we have been told by the preacher, the Bible, our parents, our church school teachers, our bosses, our political leaders, or even our husbands, wives, or children. And while we work very hard to do those things, we do them out of the fearfulness of sloth, the protected way of never accepting responsibility for our own lives.

Such sloth is a very different thing from true restfulness, which is a natural and necessary part of the rhythm of creativity. One does not avoid accidie by avoiding resting, and by working instead. One defeats it by finally seeing why it is that one rests and works without hope. Without hope for a successful outcome it is masochistic to care what happens in the world, since one knows in advance that what will happen is bad. So why care? And why try?

If you suspect yourself of slothfulness, there are some questions you can ask yourself that will help confirm or deny the accuracy of the diagnosis. First and foremost: "When you are resting, do you enjoy it?" If rest feels good, it is in the service of life and not death, and it is not sin. A second question is this: "When you finish being inactive, of your own free will and accord, do you return to your effort more able to do it well?" If you do, then your rest has served your vocation, and you should put your accusers aside. Another question: "Are you confident that you can, by your own efforts, in cooperation with the things spiritual and material that are here in the world, effect the happiness of your life?" If so, then you will make those efforts, and your adulthood is being fulfilled. When human beings have achieved adulthood, they know they can have an effect (however humble) on the world, they know they can influence their own happiness, and so they do productive work and are clear about their right to decide about their lives.

On the other hand, if your answers to the questions were negative, you may have fallen into sloth. What then? The most crucial thing to do is to recognize that life does not always have to be this way. The condition is an aberration, not the way things were meant to be for you. If you can make the decision that you will not allow yourself to continue the self-inflicted damage and the destruction of your potential any longer, then there are a number of things you can do. First, you can stop kicking yourself. Though you bear the responsibility for your own choices, and though it is an unwise and destructive situation you are in, you had help getting there, could not have done it alone, and won't be helped by punishing yourself further. In fact, meditating on the taste of your guilt will definitely make it worse. Rather, allow yourself to remember that however wrong those decisions were, at the time they were made they appeared to be the best among the options you had available. They may even have been the best, and what you have failed to notice as you grew older is that the circumstances which once made you powerless have in fact changed. Now the power to act lies within you, and the power to defeat you no longer resides in the other. It may take a psychotherapist, pastoral or otherwise, to help you correct that mistaken belief, but it is utterly crucial that you discover your own power to act.

Once that is done, the victory is closer, though it is not yet assured. It is almost certain that as you first begin to act in new fields of endeavor, you will again quickly feel guilty. The guilt operates like negative conditioning. A cat in an experimental apparatus learns not to touch the lever that zapped him with an electric shock the last five times he made contact. And it is very difficult to get the cat to touch that lever again, even if the electrical connection has been severed. Likewise, it is difficult to get you to carry through with an action that used to produce unpleasant feelings, because you expect that the same persons who disapproved before will be there to disapprove and get you to feel guilty again. In fact, you have learned it so well that you will feel guilty in their absence. Remember, that feeling of guilt is trying to reinforce in you a lie about the world: that you should not and cannot act independently and have any good come of it. Learned to disregard that inevitable feeling. Instead, learn to accept the grace that promises forgiveness even if you do blunder. If you can do this, your freedom from accidie is guaranteed. You are now ready to live as more of an adult than you have ever been.

# 3. Gluttony — Overindulgence

As sloth is the childhood sin growing from infants' proper restfulness and improper sense that they can't change their world, gluttony is the counterpart that stems from children's immense appetite for food, stimulation, and experience. Eating is what infants do when not sleeping. Parents of very young children are at their happiest when their children are eating everything they are supposed to and sleeping as much as possible when not eating. We would not accuse an infant of gluttony, any more than of sloth. It is when those immense appetites persist into later childhood and beyond that we think of them as problematic; and when they dominate an adult, the title of sin is fully appropriate.

For most children, eating is not a problem. You make available a selection of foods to them, and they will eat what they want and need and will quit eating when full. Children have a natural controlling mechanism that lets them know when they need to eat and when they need to stop; how much they need to eat to give the body what it requires to grow; and how they need to regulate what they eat in order to maintain and properly increase their weight.

This natural control apparently extends throughout human life and the rest of the animal kingdom. You will never see a wild animal grown fat. Researchers have found that rats and other animals have a sensing mechanism in their brains that lets them know when they have eaten enough to maintain their present weight. When that amount has been reached, the rat will stop eating. It is possible experimentally to confuse the rat in a variety of ways, but if its brain is intact and its present weight is one at which it can function, it will not get fatter, nor, in the presence of adequate food and good health, will it get thinner. There is no reason to believe that this same automatic regulatory mechanism does not operate in every animal as complex as the rat.

The problem of gluttony lies in the fact that we are a great deal more complex than the rat. We have the ability to override the internal signals that tell us to stop eating (drinking, exercising, reading, and everything else). We override those signals by telling ourselves we need and want more, or less, than we do; by accepting social situations that put others in a position to regulate when we start and stop; and by having other legitimately competing wants. Some of us learn to override so well that we are not even aware of the original signal we are choosing to ignore. An ironic result is that we can overuse the ability to discipline ourselves to not eat (or do) what we want right now, and can gradually lose our ability to regulate ourselves naturally. To put it another way, too much discipline, too early, makes us dependent on being externally disciplined thereafter and leaves us unable to respond to predisciplinary ways of being sure that we get what we need and no more.

That produces inevitable conflict, since it is obvious that a completely inner-regulated person, especially a young child, is not very compatible with any social situation of which he or she is not dictator. It is essential to override some of those impulses, and to teach children to override them themselves, if they are going to live in reasonable peace with each other. It is not possible to overcome the danger of too much overriding by not overriding at all, since that produces anarchy. There will inevitably be times for all young children when they won't want any more roast beef because they are so eager for the ice cream. There will even be times when they don't have the patience for the ice cream, even when they haven't had enough to eat, because they want to go play with their friends. And there will certainly be times when you want your children to eat something more now, because you want them not to get hungry in the middle of the ball game, the funeral, the drive to grandmother's, or whatever it is you are going to do next. There will even be times when you want them to take one more helping and get really sleepy, because you just don't have the emotional energy to deal with their wanting affection from you. And even if that doesn't happen, your children will learn by themselves that they don't feel as bad about the puppy that ran away this morning if they can have one more piece of chocolate cake. In all of those situations the children are learning that there are times when they prefer not to pay attention to the body's natural signals of hunger or not-hunger, and in all of those they are laying the groundwork for the later ability to fall into gluttony.

There are some particularly dangerous situations affecting our ability to regulate ourselves, and they typically produce people who are most deeply enslaved to gluttony. Most of our parents really wanted us as children to learn to eat when we were hungry and stop when we were full; to initiate a new activity when we were bored and quit when we got tired; to enjoy a glass of wine at a family gathering and stop when we began to feel a little different from usual. But some parents, usually without knowing it, don't value such self-regulation very much at all. If you grew up with that sort of parent, you probably had experiences of saying things like, "Mommy, my throat hurts," and having mommy say back, "No it doesn't." I came to know one such child in his chronological adulthood. When he was ten years old, his mother died. He was crying over her death when his father came up to him, slapped him across the face, and told him

to stop that crying because there were things that needed
to be done now. As you might imagine, this same child had
been expected to systematically ignore all the signals that
came from his body about what he wanted to do. When he
broke three fingers in a playground accident, it was not his
pain that was responded to, but his having carelessly caused
an inconvenience for the family. On less dramatic occasions, at any point where the child became noticeably angry
with either parent, he was hit. The same child is now forty
years old and weighs over three hundred pounds. This boy
had learned that there were ways he could provide comfort
for himself in the midst of a family experience that was
almost wholly unresponsive to his needs. Further, his family
actively encouraged him to pay little attention to those
needs, so it was a very natural way of gaining comfort to
ignore his body's signals about being stuffed with food.
That became more complicated for him when, by middle
childhood, his family began to feel that his increasing fat-
ness was an embarrassment to them, and would regularly
demand that he eat less. By this time his body had become
accustomed to eating more, and he had become accustomed to being very angry with his family. Since his eating
was very difficult for them to control, he could use it as a
regular way to remind them that there was one area of his
life they were not going to be allowed to manage.

The personal consequences of this situation for the glutton are obvious. This man, for example, though he holds a
graduate degree in communications, has never held the
kind of job he wants and for which he is trained. He typically
will be employed for a few months in some degradingly
nonprofessional situation, then be unemployed for a few
months, building up sizable debts, then stay humiliatingly
employed for about long enough to pay off those debts
before somebody finds some reason for not wanting him
around. Since this is not an unusual way for society to respond to the fat person, he can count on the pattern con-

tinuing unless he gains some control over his body. What is also obvious, of course, is that he won't have to worry about the pattern continuing too long, because he will die perhaps twenty years earlier than he would were he of normal weight. Gluttony is that sin of which the wages are most certainly death, and that rather quickly. It is also not surprising that this man hasn't had a date in his life and will probably finish his life without ever having established a close relationship with a woman, having had children, or being able to pass along whatever he learned of life to a family. Relationally he is impoverished, there being only a small number of people who don't, after a time, find his regular suicidal activity with knife and fork to be so personally painful that they find excuses for avoiding his company —despite the fact that this is an intelligent and cultured man who is not unpleasant to be with, as long as you don't notice what he's doing to himself and care about it.

Though this situation is both a tragic and an intelligible one, it is also one that my friend has the capability and responsibility to either change or claim as his preferred way of dealing with what life has offered him. We probably can't hold him responsible for having been fat at five, but he surely bears a share of responsibility for having been obese at twenty and every day thereafter. Gluttony for him became a chosen way when he failed to notice the opportunities that increasing age makes available to us all to gain our gratifications in less destructive ways. At some point we move from the senseless tragedy of being raised by blind and selfish parents, into the sinful responsibility of having perpetuated a painful childhood through a period of life that in principle had a different potential. As a result, some of the hope for God's creation has been lost; this person's creativity will never be fully available to the world; his ugliness will ever force others to choose between denying themselves the pleasure of his enlightened conversation and denying the importance of their own aesthetic judgments; and his life may well have been squandered.

Let's move now from the obvious disaster that the sin of gluttony can produce in the life of one man to a more formal look at what it is in general. "Gluttony" is defined here as that motivation which leads us to disregard our own innate self-regulation and take into ourselves more of a substance or experience than we would naturally want for its own sake.

Gluttony deals with much more than food. Food is only the most obvious of the potentially infinite list of things that can be misused in a gluttonous way. For instance, drunkenness has traditionally been listed as a category of gluttony. A number of other overconsumptions can be so classified. One can read too much, stay awake too long, walk too far, work too hard, play too much bridge, or see too many people—all because of this basic self-created flaw in our ways of regulating ourselves.

With food and drink the results are more obvious, but consider for a moment the case of a person who is gluttonous about hiking. I know such a man well. He looked at a map the other day, saw that he could take a short and easy trail in a state park with his wife, and that he would have perhaps sixty to ninety minutes' worth of energy and space in their schedule to hike a more difficult trail alone. There were two such trails shown on the map, each with some distinctive characteristics, and he found it hard to choose between them. So he put them together into a package, started happily on the first leg of his journey, but by mid-trip found himself exhausted, satiated with beautiful wilderness that he was now too tired to see, and worried about meeting his schedule with his wife. By the time the hike was finished, he was very nearly late, too tired to be worth anything, and had really wasted his experience of the last part of the trail because he was so full of natural beauty that his sensitivity was exhausted. He would have enjoyed half the walk better than he enjoyed all of it.

Another form of gluttony that is particularly life-sapping

for able people is the preoccupation with that which one is not doing because one is doing what one is doing. Because I am writing this book, I am busy and I can't be simultaneously writing another book I have in mind. Because I am painting the house, I can't be reading that great novel I want to read. There is a pressure in some of us to be taking in more experience than we can take in at a time, with the result that the reality and enjoyment of the actual present experience is lost. I can't enjoy anything because I'm not now consuming (doing) everything. This malady is especially prevalent in people who see themselves as having to make up for lost time—and who of us hasn't lost time in regard to some experience in our lives that we want? So when we finally have it open to us, whether it's enough money or good food or sexual freedom or a fine library, we find it difficult not to try to make up for what we didn't enjoy yesterday—by trying to enjoy more today than our organism has room for. We expect to have a full head of steam for devouring superb French cooking when we hit New Orleans, and we fail to notice that by the evening of the second day our body is screaming for a plain, unadulterated head of lettuce. To eat another magnificent shrimp creation in a perfect creole sauce, in that situation, is gluttony. Eating it the night before may have been an appropriate celebration of the goodness of creation.

One can read a lot of garbage about gluttony. You can find books that will tell you that anytime you have a second helping of mashed potatoes or even a first of red meat, your sin is approaching the level of unforgivability. You can also be told that to know the difference between a good wine and a poor one is prima facie evidence that the devil already has his snare around you. I don't believe either of those, and that's not just because I don't want to. It is part of the natural rhythm of life to alternate between occasional magnificent excesses of self-indulgence, which remind us that this really is a rich and good world, and longer, ordinary periods of eating bologna sandwiches and Hamburger Helper. It is also part of being an intelligent human being to know what really does give you sensual pleasure and what you would just as soon do without. What is gluttonous is to fail to heed the natural, i.e., God-given, awareness that enough is enough.

It should be obvious from this that gluttony, like sloth, is not the sole possession of those unfortunate few whose lives are totally ruined by it. It is there in all of us at those occasional moments when something bids us to ignore our own most natural wantings. Each time we heed that something, we deprive ourselves of the joy that is actually to be had in life through the mistaken belief that what we are doing now holds the greatest source of happiness that we can presently reach, and should be continued forever. This is the Faustian sin: "Stay! Thou art so fair." No matter what the joy, our bodies know (even if our souls do not) that if the bidden object were to stay forever, we would soon tire of it; our involvement would become more a joyless addiction or dependence than a freely offered gift.

Unfortunately, the results of gluttony are not limited to the ruined individual lives of a few grotesque examples, nor even to the personal embarrassments it gives all of us from time to time. We live in a world in which consumption of almost every physical resource is accelerating at a rate that cannot possibly be continued. If those who cannot read this book because they are illiterate or because they cannot speak its language were suddenly rich enough to be able to consume at the level of those who can, there would not be the resources in the world at this moment to support the resulting level of consumption. Even if the resources do not run out—and they may—we in the Western world can continue to enjoy our accustomed satisfactions only because those in other parts of the world cannot bid higher for the available goods.

I would not want to trace all the evils of the world's

income distribution to gluttony, but it certainly is a contributor to the evil, along with avarice and envy. That is true especially in our culture, because we have learned how to consume to avoid feeling. When we as a people are faced with a crisis that will hurt immediately if we pay attention to it, we are generally able to divert ourselves by introducing some new experience, consuming some new good, and thereby not feel the sting that would otherwise come. In my therapeutic work I am especially reminded of the availability of that escape to the very wealthy, who have readily available the option of putting on a new dress or going out to a fine meal, instead of sitting at home and being aware of how uncomfortable it is when their relationships are not working. This is one of the dangers of wealth, not because the wealthy are intrinsically evil, but because the ability to consume in large quantities disguises the typical limitations that pain brings with it for most people. Gluttony is a special danger to those who have the financial ability to be gluttonous.

Compared to many in the world, Americans are well off. As a rich people, we have learned well to divert ourselves with new experiences rather than cope with the difficulties inside us. That leaves us in an inescapable tension between our wish to be at peace with the world and our need to keep consuming at a level other nations cannot possibly approach—unless they deprive us of our most familiar and trusted ways of keeping ourselves comfortable. The recent power of the petroleum-exporting countries makes it clear that the avoidance of that tension may be a luxury we cannot long afford. We may have to decide between keeping our gluttony—at the price of going to war with the innocent—and giving up our gluttony and being left open to the discomforts that come to us when this handy diversion is lost.

One element of gluttony that I have not touched on, but that is a feature in almost every instance, is the belief that "if I don't consume it now, it won't be here to consume later." It seems to come from the experience as a child of finding there was not enough—enough love, enough food, enough freedom—which led to a fear of being left without any at all. The illusion that goes along with this fear is that if I continue to eat (or drink, love, read, play, etc.) beyond the point where I have had enough for now, there will somehow be some of it left over inside me. It is as though I will be able to delay being hungry for love tomorrow if I take a double portion today. There is some reality to that, especially when one is dealing with physical commodities, but only some. I am not as likely to starve to death tomorrow if I overeat today, or to feel sexually frustrated tomorrow if I completely exhaust all my sexual responsiveness today. But the extension of that principle beyond very basic physical needs—and the extension even in those areas beyond a short term and limited sense—is always false. When I do want to make love again, I will want it just as much regardless of how many times or with how many partners I did it the last time. If three months from now I shall have been without food for a whole month, it will matter very little that I have gorged myself today.

The addictions present a special case of gluttony. There is a difference between them and the remaining forms. Systematic overindulgence in alcohol, marijuana, or any other drug is at first motivated in exactly the same way that overindulgence in food or hiking or any other gratifying experience is. What is different is that, because of the particular biological fit between our bodies and the molecules of heroin, THC, alcohol, etc., the effects of that overindulgence are multiplied many times in vulnerable individuals. For those same persons, unfortunately, the sense of felt need for the escape provided by the drug is typically greatest. A bitter struggle is set off between internal and external forces that are demanding the drug and those that would refrain. For these persons the need is greater and so is the penalty for gratifying it. They are not any more evil than the rest of us, at least to begin with, but the results of their indulging these personal and private vices are much more far-reaching, and often become public. That in turn gives the rest of us a greater stake in controlling their indulgence, and it explains the zeal with which our prohibitionist forebears tried to eradicate the evil of drink. The problem, both then and now, was not in the drink or even in the drinking, but in the combination of inattention to the physical signals that one has had enough, and the choice to escape whatever pain led to the drinking becoming excessive, habitual, and dangerous.

The problem with addiction, whether alcoholism or any other, is that discovering the cause and removing the initial reasons the person became addicted will not change the person's continued vulnerability to the drug. An alcoholic will still be alcoholic even if he knows he started because his father beat him. At the point where addiction begins, the motivation for gluttony shifts from whatever original pain the addict escaped via the drug, to the wish to escape the pain of being without the substance to which one is addicted. It remains an escape, but an escape from such a powerful and threatening force that it feels like the temporary introduction of a perfect bliss. At this point every new dose of the drug deepens the addiction, compounds the sin, and makes it harder to heal. It may not be gluttonous or sinful for you or me to have a drink after dinner, but if an alcoholic is your dinner guest, and drinks with you, it becomes a different matter.

As with most sins that we wish to manage, our typical collective impulse is to avoid or prohibit something. This has been much of the Protestant response to alcohol. And were prohibition ever possible, it might do a lot to eliminate the bad effects connected with overdrinking. But it would not eliminate gluttony of other commodities as a sin to which the same persons would remain highly vulnerable. They would substitute other addictions, preferably more benign ones, but life would only be whole for them with the devotion of a substantial effort toward satisfying their emotional starvation. Since that is the same challenge as confronts any recovering alcoholic today, prohibition doesn't hold any decisive promise for the abuser. What it obviously does offer is a lot of inconvenience and pain for people who use alcohol more responsibly, as well as a huge opportunity for malignant members of our society to take control of the illegal ways in which people get liquor.

As the redemption of the slothful cannot be effected solely by getting them up and making them work, so the redemption of gluttons cannot be achieved by simply forcing them to stop consuming. What will effect it must begin with a greater understanding of what these sinners need so desperately that they are willing to shut off their own natural signals about when to stop. If you can ascertain what is needed, you often can help the glutton to find it and thereby to get some freedom from the gluttony.

I said earlier that slothful persons would often win the psychiatric label of depression. Gluttons, in the severest forms of their affliction, would typically be seen as suffering from a character disorder, usually of the narcissistic variety. They have been wounded deeper and earlier in life than the slothful. The slothful usually have at least had the experience of some times in which they did feel good, though such times were typically achieved only by doing what another person or persons had first indicated they wanted. The others were willing to provide what would make the slothful one feel good, in exchange for getting their way.

Gluttons have not been so fortunate. Typically no one knew or cared what would make them feel good, and the only way they could get distinctly good feelings was in a completely isolated, selfish act—eating. For gluttons, food is only an object to be consumed. There is a wound, a pain flowing from the lack of a satisfaction that cannot be found in the glutton's world. Gluttons find a substitute, typically food (but it can be anything), and overdose on it beyond the point where the body sends signals that say stop. To have heard those signals as a child would have meant to abandon the only way of avoiding a misery that could be found at any of a thousand moments. Gluttons deeply care that they stop feeling miserable, thus being in a sense the opposite of the slothful, who appear to care little about most things. Gluttons hurt more deeply, crave relief more desperately, and identify more keenly with the hurts of others. But they typically do not know what makes the other hurt or have much trust in their ability to improve the other's lot or their own.

For gluttons there comes a time in life when the actual childhood inability to find a safe environment for hearing their own internal signals is over. A new person might enter their life, they might grow up and leave home, their parents might change. But to the extent that they are committed gluttons, they will rely so thoroughly on the one means they know of being comfortable that they will neither see nor use the opportunity produced by the change. At that moment the sin begins unquestionably to be sin. But gluttons are already deeply limited in their ability to escape gluttony, because the internal signals that could tell them when they were full have been systematically dulled by years of inattention; and the ways of responding healthily to those signals have never been developed at all. No alternate behaviors to consuming have been learned.

If you often find yourself doing more of something than you really want to, and nobody else is forcing you to do it, you are probably a victim of the sin of gluttony. What can you do? The cure must begin, as with sloth, not by trying to zealously avoid the sin, but by listening intently to the pain the sin is trying to drown out. Be aware of what and when you really want to consume, and when you want it, consume it—whether it be a chocolate pie, a Brahms concerto, or a beautiful hiking trail. But consume it only up to the point where you stop wanting it. The temptation will be to keep eating, reading, walking, or whatever, because you know that doing it up to this moment has been pleasant. The trick is to stop now and allow yourself to be vulnerable to the uneasiness that will develop because you don't know what to do next, and because you do know that it may not be as satisfying as eating that last bite was in the previous moment.

It is the mastery of that moment that holds the key to freedom from gluttony. It is inevitably a frightening instant, because you are faced with the necessity of satisfying yourself and you have no established, proven, way to do it. Again, the only safety is in listening to your body and your soul. What do you want to do right now besides retreating to the tired, familiar slavery that produces a final outcome you do not like? Your body, with its various itches and twitches and tensions, will often suggest that right now what you want is to move around, or lie down, or hold someone, or throw pillows at the wall, or any of a thousand things. Do what it suggests, if it seems safe to yourself and the surroundings. Often the idea will come from your imagination. Suddenly a vision may appear of an activity that looks like fun. Find it and indulge. Very, very often we try to tell ourselves what is the next thing to do, but we miss our own message.

There will be many obstacles along that path, because almost all the things that a glutton first would want to do, he or she doesn't yet know how to do. It may be asking for a date, or writing a poem, or shooting baskets, or going roller-skating, or fixing the roof. The only thing we can know about it for sure is that it will be a new thing for that person in that situation, because it won't be the old familiar solution that has never worked but has always been tried before. And, typically, our sinner is especially sensitive to embarrassment about making a fool of himself or herself by doing something badly. The only escape lies in facing that embarrassment and learning to do well enough for you the thing your body and your imagination are telling you to do. You may have to practice a thousand times with no one looking, or tell yourself over and over again to stop your own self-criticism, but you must remember that the only way to get acceptably good at whatever it is, is to do it over and over again until you eliminate your mistakes. Only then can it become a source of gratification that can compete with too much food or drink, and thus become the first reliable bridge out of a lifetime of slavery to the most certainly—even physically—deadly of the sins.

# PART III

# *The Sins of Prolonged Adolescence*

---

# 4. Anger — Vengefulness

The ability to feel anger and act angrily begins very early, but in most people it only reaches its full effectiveness and greatest danger with the physical and psychological growth of adolescence. During those transition years, anger aids the delicate and vital work of becoming an individual; but both during and after this crucial effort it remains a tricky and dangerous tool, one that readily tempts us to the sin of vengefulness.

The ability to be angry, a physiological state marked by rapid heart rate, increased blood flow to the peripheral muscles, and increased physical strength, is a God-given capacity that has been vital to our survival as a species for millennia. Every one of us first experiences it before we are able to speak, on those inevitable occasions when father or mother is not quite as quick with the milk or the dry diaper or the comforting hand as we would like. We scream and shout and thrash around, having no idea of anything else we might do to relieve our powerless need for the other person, who is not moving as quickly as our discomfort tells us he or she ought to be. Unless that experience reinforces itself by piling up new occurrences before the old ones are finished, it will subside quickly on each repetition when the comforting parent arrives and calms us. Our anger then has brought us help.

By the time we reach the age of two or three and can move

around freely and half express ourselves in our limited vocabularies, our anger has inevitably added a dimension of power; in turn it is complicated by the fear that we will be snuffed out as individuals for merely asserting the right to be separate persons, or for doing it in a way different from what our parents had hoped for. Each such frustration, for a few pivotal hours, brings a crushing blow to our vision of ourselves as free and powerful, producing a rage we can only barely control. The rage in turn leads to fear, and for a time we vacillate between self-confident grandiose power and the intense longing to be exactly what mommy and daddy want us to be. If we do not succumb to the latter and give way to a lifelong pattern of sloth, and if we are fortunate enough to have parents who will tolerate the storms without throwing us down the stairs, we survive to become three, and to begin testing our environment and learning our world in ways that will prepare us to have the freedom our dawning sense of individuality is pushing us toward.

When that learning is well along, and when physical size enables a certain degree of self-protection, and when the societal pressures externally and the sexual pressures internally begin to demand a fuller self-definition, we find ourselves in the normal period of temporary insanity termed adolescence. Its onset will be marked by the no-longer-child's angry response to a request for assistance that yesterday would simply have produced assistance. Though its beginnings are sporadic and not clearly marked off, and though some children become adolescents once and for all overnight and others flirt with beginning it for five or even fifteen years, it eventually comes to everyone who has not made a permanent life decision in favor of sloth.

The inner experience of the person becoming adolescent, when hearing that request for help with the garbage, is totally unlike what it had been the previous day when he or she was a child. Yesterday it went like this: "They want me to empty the garbage, doing what they want has usually worked out for me before; I'm not doing anything particularly important anyway; I want them to like me and be nice to me; so I'll empty the garbage." Today it's a completely different ball game: "I'm doing something really exciting that I've just figured out will make me happy; if I don't do it right now my chance to do it and get that happiness will be gone forever; I'm finally old enough to accomplish that sort of thing for myself; my God, I can't possibly stop now; if I do that, they'll be running my life and I've just figured out that it's up to me to run my life; besides, what would my friends think?" The result is that if the garbage gets emptied, it happens only after substantial unpleasantness between parent and adolescent, and often after they figure out a way to make peace with this new sense of self. Both parties end up paying quite a bit for the difference.

Anger plays a vital role in this change. Our culture demands that we leave home and establish some independence by a certain age; and it won't allow us easy access to some of the greater pleasures of life until that is accomplished. But being dependent and safe at home is a poor stimulus to getting on with leaving, and it is hardest of all when you are getting along beautifully with the other people there. It's practically mandatory to be angry if you are going to separate at all. The probability of anger is helped along by the fact that parents can't possibly know the precise moment at which you are no longer a child and feel ready to claim sovereignty over a given piece of your life. But you know, and expect your parent to know; so that the first parental request that comes after you have crossed that invisible boundary feels to you like an unwarranted trespassing on your own territory. To your parent, the resulting angry response is likely to come as a substantial surprise, since yesterday it was all right to ask you to take out the garbage. A parent who is up to the task will not let the newly-become-adolescent escape taking out the garbage simply because the adolescent is angry, and that will stir up a feeling in the adolescent of being oppressed. That produces distance between child and parent, and in that distance the child begins to imagine a world without a parent in it to request that the garbage be taken out. In that imagination the child, it is hoped, has a place for taking out the garbage on his or her own schedule, which presumably will be a little different from that of the parent. Sometimes the garbage does have to get pretty deep.

This anger is inevitable at hundreds or thousands of points as the transitional years unfold. Depending on the parent's strength, the child may exaggerate the anger to become dictator of the family; or the child may stifle the anger upon learning that to show anger is very dangerous; or the child can play a middle course that leads to a fully individuated adulthood. At many points the new adolescent will feel a strong sense of pride and triumph at having won one more chunk of territory from mom and dad; and with it will come the sense of now being able to organize another sphere of life without fear of the interruptions that can throw off one's plans and reabsorb a person into the world of childhood. This is an appropriate and joyous celebration, for parenting is not completed until that competence is achieved.

But this story line can go awry. One of the detours was explored in the chapter on sloth, so I'll only remind you that some children find it so dangerous to be angry (an essential part of individuation) that they permanently abandon their right to independent judgment. But those we are most concerned with in this chapter have learned too well that the fastest way to get what they want from their parents is through anger. Parent and child have colluded to create a situation in which the child can be chronically angry. In it the child can feel justified, strong, commanding, and in control of a freedom that can't be obtained in any other way. Of course, most of the child's feelings represent inaccurate perceptions, but it will be many years before the chronically angry person is fully aware of that.

It is at this point that the transition between the natural and often healthy feeling of anger, and the unnecessary and destructive sin of vengefulness, occurs. That event takes place when the enjoyment of being angry blinds the adolescent to information that would indicate whether he or she still needs to be angry to maintain the growth toward independent selfhood. It is very easy at this time in life to take anger as the major building block of identity, so that it would feel strange and weak not to be angry. But inevitably there comes a point in the process where the parent has decided to give up control of the area in question, and to allow the emerging adult to take responsibility for that part of life. It is very rare for the youngster to recognize that decision at the moment it happens, just as it was very rare for the parent to determine the earlier point when the child had decided to be the boss of that function.

Some parents never do give up, and are constantly attempting to coerce their grown children's behavior as long as they live. They make it especially attractive for their children to be vengeful, since it often is lost on those grown children that the parent's ability to compel behavior ended many years ago. Once you have felt enslaved by another person, you are almost always on guard against any attempt to reinstate that enslavement, even if you ought to know that you are strong enough to prevent it without having to be angry.

A man I knew a number of years ago illustrated this transition beautifully. His father was a welder, owned his own business, and combined in his own character a demanding criticalness with the ability to practically forget that he had a son except when the two of them were together, which was not often, as he was very busy. When they were together the put-downs were constant, and when the boy wanted him around, there was no way to get it to happen. For good or ill he got enough reassurance from his mother so that he did not choose the route of sloth, but instead nursed a sullen, quiet anger until he reached such a size that his father couldn't back up threatening words with physical punishments. In the meantime, the boy avoided his father as much as possible, and especially avoided making any attempts to do difficult things when his father was close enough to ridicule his failures.

But once his size was achieved, the boy made a decision that all this was going to change. One day the father criticized his form shooting baskets in the backyard and the boy told his dad what he could do with his criticism. It was pungent. Part of the message was that he didn't want the old man telling him that he was a dummy. If he started it, the son promised he would point out some of his failings he had noticed over the years. To that point, the son's outburst may have been necessary for him to become an individual human being, but what happened over the next twenty years was not. The boy had made his point, though the father didn't like it. The criticism, at least audibly, stopped; and the father resolved to keep as close to the edges of his son's life as safety would allow. But for the next twenty years their every contact was marked by the son's wounding the older man at least once with a remark about how he would no longer let the father control him, about what a superior person he (the son) was, and how much reparation was still owed him. The father died with the offenses on both sides still unforgiven, so the son will bear the scar of his vengefulness for the rest of his life. He could have seen the change of his father's heart, but was seduced by the pleasure in his anger and the safety in keeping his father at such a distance that no change was possible.

The sin in this story was not the anger, but the decision to continue using the anger to power the production of pain. There is a crucial distinction here between emotion and attitude. An emotion is a physical state, arising out of the body, measurable by physical means, and more or less involuntary in its first appearance in any situation. It is the way our bodies tell us what situation we are in. Anger is an emotion. An attitude is a stance we take toward the world, or a part of it, that determines our behavior. It may be conscious or unconscious, but it is always capable of being made conscious if a person is sufficiently introspective and has the right help.

People take many things into account in forming their attitudes, and one of those things is emotion. But there is no direct causal link between a given emotion and an attitude. Indeed, one piece of the attitude is a decision about what one is going to do with the emotion.

Vengefulness is an attitude, and insofar as that attitude is expressed in behavior, it is sin. It is the decision that I will act on my anger by trying to hurt the person with whom I am angry. But I can also make a different decision about my very real anger, one that would not be sinful. The crux of the matter is that we choose the attitude, after a certain point in maturation, but that the feeling comes unbidden.

It is possible for you to structure your life so that the chance for specific feelings to come up is diminished; and once a particular feeling makes its appearance it is possible over a matter of minutes or seconds to modify it, but it is not possible to utterly prevent its appearance. So it is not reasonable to call the appearance of the feeling of "anger" sin.

Though the Bible and the Christian tradition have been very mixed in their treatment of anger, there are at least two Scripture verses that support the distinction made here. Paul wrote to his followers, "Be angry, but sin not." The issue for Paul was not the emotion, not even its expression, but the intent and effect they had. Again, quoting from Moses and the combined wisdom of the Hebrews, Paul wrote, "Vengeance is mine, I will repay, saith the Lord," an acknowledgment that the human attempt to settle past accounts will not produce holy results.

I define "vengefulness" as the decision, conscious or otherwise, to attempt to cause pain or damage to the object of my anger. I can be angry with you, yet choose to use my anger in a way that benefits both of us, such as by resolving the conflict between us. Such a use of anger is not vengeful and is not sin. But I can also choose to use it in belittling you in a way that I know will make you unhappy, to plot against you to deprive you of social position or material goods, or to lash out physically against you in an attempt to leave you either injured or dead. All of the latter are unambiguously sinful.

It seems unnecessary to detail the dangers of vengefulness to the well-being of the individual and her or his world. Probably nothing fills the average person with horror as quickly as imagining someone's sudden anger leaving oneself or one's loved ones dead or seriously injured.

Both the doer and the object of the vengefulness are inescapably damaged. The target is wounded, materially or socially, by the intent of the doer; and the vengeful doer incurs both guilt and retribution. A person who (like a sociopath) is temperamentally so poorly connected with other people that others' feelings do not seem very real may avoid guilt. Some persons can also be schooled to rationalize away their guilt, or be desensitized to it by so much exposure that it becomes meaningless, as in the case of the professional soldier or the guard in the concentration camp. But though guilt can in many cases be stilled or made meaningless, the danger of retribution remains.

Vengefulness always includes with it an element of overkill, a disproportion between the original offense and the retaliation. People who are hit with it feel the disproportion, feel the injustice, and are in turn left with a wrong that they feel they must right, which spurs their attack on the originally vengeful person. Even if the other is too weak to be a threat, there is no way to remove the possibility that he or she may have allies who are strong, or that the situation may change so that the one who is strong now will be weaker or more vulnerable later. Vengefulness sets up an unstable situation, inevitably increasing the chances of punishment from outside, and very often producing a painful inner punishment as well.

The relational dangers of vengefulness can likewise be damning beyond belief. I sat once with a vengeful couple. The man was complaining that he had been trying to get his wife to want sex for the duration of their thirty-year marriage, but five years before had decided he had had enough rejection and was never again going to approach her sexually or welcome her approach. He had been true to that commitment, and in his vengefulness had shut off all touch, all statements of affection, all sense of joint ownership in property or children—but insisted on remaining in the home and calling himself married. She, victim of her own slothfulness, had finally been reduced to the point where she was so desperate for some affirmation that she asked me to help her get it from him. She had, in the meantime, become as vengeful toward him as he was toward her, so that any attempt either made toward the other was scorned as false, dishonest, and dangerous. Unless our work was more successful than I think, both of these persons are likely to spend the next twenty years seeing their lives defined by a marriage that has become worse than a desert, and watching their children live out those vengeful miseries in their own well-learned ways.

Even less needs to be said about the danger when women and men of this vengeful spirit gain national leadership, and are pressed to maintain that spirit by the vengefulness of their supporters. In a world that has seen the slaughter of who knows how many Jews, Russians, Cambodians, Vietnamese, Nicaraguans, and American blacks; that has feared the repetition of the horrors of Hiroshima and Nagasaki; and that wonders realistically if it is safe to invest a billion dollars in health insurance rather than in a new missile system, the hideous destructiveness of this particular sin on a global scale needs no explanation.

But how can we organize our lives so that we don't fall victim to it? With the other sins our response has been to look for the basic wish hiding under the offense, to see if there is another way it can be satisfied. This is more complex with vengefulness than most, because many wishes are expressed through it. But once we have discarded those we could regard as expressive of other sins, like envy, pride, and avarice, two wishes stand out that we traditionally have honored as Christians: the wish for safety and the wish for personal freedom.

Those two wishes together leave us in very complex and difficult situations, for as Jean-Paul Sartre pointed out, the freedom of the other is perpetually a threat to my freedom and my safety. As long as I cannot be assured that you will not interfere with my attempts to get what I want, I must at least toy with the possibility of restricting your freedom and safety so you will not restrict mine. You know that also and will be on guard against me, setting up a situation where it is easy to assume that restriction is what you want for me. If I make that assumption, which is the adolescent assumption in the beginning, the only way I can stop you from damaging me is either to control you perfectly or to damage you so thoroughly that you lose the power to damage me. We are then in a situation where safety and freedom are very tenuously available, where vengefulness is a constant temptation, and where the possibility of having perfect safety is open to considerable doubt.

Human beings have tried a number of ways to achieve safety and freedom. Here are three of the most common variants.

1. "I'm the king of the castle, and you're the dirty rascal." This is the traditional method, attempted by those who thought they had the power to pull it off. It is vengefulness in its fullest corporate development, and it requires my

commitment to be stronger than anyone else and to regard anyone who is developing his or her own strength as a potential enemy whose attempt must be undermined so that I can remain safe. The underlying belief here is that I am safe and can be free only so long as I am stronger than you. If your strength is approaching mine, you are automatically the enemy, because one of the rules is that nobody is allowed to get nearly as strong as I. The assumption is that if you do get as strong as I, you will try to kill me off so you can be king of the castle. Since I have been acting toward you all along in such an unlovable way, I have probably increased the likelihood that you will do exactly that.

My vengefulness has created or nurtured your will to retaliate. Therefore, I have good reason to be frightened of you in the event that you should become strong enough to be a danger to me. Examples of this can be found just about anywhere you look. It is a very prevalent situation in families like that of the young rebel I described above, where the father is insecure about his authority and so views every development in his son's strength as a danger. It is commonly felt in business, where it becomes second nature for the middle manager who is getting a little long in the tooth to suspect the bright young guy in the next office of being after his job. Its international and political consequences are obvious and widespread. The present relationship between the United States and the Soviet Union is an example of this, as each believes that the only reason the other would be trying to become strong is to try to destroy its rival. The paramount example of this way of functioning is to be found in the internal politics of country after country where a violent revolution has overthrown the former regime, to be replaced by one just as suspicious and brutal as the previous one, which is in turn overthrown for the sake of the freedom of the people, and so on indefinitely. Iran is a classic example of this, as was Chile in the early 1970s and Cuba a decade before that. It should be noted that this was precisely the attitude of Hitler that led directly to the death of six million Jews.

2. "Yes sir, yes sir, three bags full." This is the classic stance of minority people who have learned to survive in societies that are ruled by folks playing king of the castle. The basic line goes like this: "Anything you say, massa, anything you say." The assumption is that if we appear to do anything our masters want us to, they won't kill us; and we're free to think anything we like about them behind their back. This is the basic political stance of sloth, and it creates a situation in which I try to buy safety at the expense of outward freedom, while maintaining the inner freedom to ridicule the very person who guarantees my safety. It creates a great deal of suspicion and hostility on the part of the "yes sir" players. It produces an unreal sense of superiority and security on the part of the "kings," and it ensures instant retaliation if any "yes sir" player gives obvious or subtle signs that he or she no longer intends to play by the rules. Thousands of southern lynchings throughout the last century have taught that lesson well. But on the other hand, the game has usually worked: if you are willing to give up enough freedom, you can have your safety.

It should be noted that this was the attitude on the part of the Jews that allowed them to be slaughtered by the millions. Increasingly it is coming to the attention of Jew and Christian alike that "yes sir" players bear some responsibility for the ultimate outcome, if they have cooperated with the myth that the king has the right to vengefully control the game.

3. This option has developed so recently that I don't have a catch phrase for it, but it is characterized by the attempt to create a world in which people sense themselves to be equal with one another. This is not to say that there will be no difference in powers, resources, abilities, or outcomes, but that I have just as much, neither more nor less, right to be treated as a human being, with full dignity in the sight

of God, as you do. This stance contends that I am in as much danger, if you begin to feel overpowered, as I am if I allow myself to be overpowered, since in either case basic distrust of the other is inevitable. It attempts to challenge the belief that somebody has to be in charge here, at least if that myth intends that it be the same somebody all the time. It holds that there can be the greatest safety and the greatest freedom for everyone if each has enough power to affect the other's behavior, and everybody knows it.

"King of the castle" is the typical life stance of the over-grown adolescent grasping authority and fearing that to allow anyone else to have as much will cause the loss of it. It is basically vengeful. "Yes sir, yes sir, three bags full" is essentially childish in that one gives up one's right to independent decisions in exchange for the emotional and physical safety which that purchases. It is essentially slothful. The third position, which seeks a world of equals, is essentially an adult stance that has the possibility of being loving.

Let us return our attention to the adolescent for a moment. He or she is angry, having just found a new treasure, freedom, and expecting—since no one ever made it available before—that as soon as adults notice it, they will try to take it away and return the young person to slavery. The adolescent is rightly angry in the face of that prospect, if his or her perception of the world is accurate. The anger is based partly on the fear that if the adult world tries to remove the adolescent's freedom, it will succeed.

Now, let's experimentally remove that fear. Let's say that you, the adolescent, have developed the competence to hold your own in the struggle with those who formerly were your superiors, and that you know it. If you know it, your need and motivation for anger diminish, and so do those of your parents. As parents we don't get nearly so angry at the stubborn two-year-old, because we know that in the long run we will win that one. But with the adolescent we are not so sure, and it is that fear and outrage which turn our anger (and that of the adolescent) into retaliatory vengefulness and threaten the stability of the entire structure. If adolescents *know* that they can maintain their freedom even if adults attempt to take it away, then any attempt that does come can be met with appropriate anger that provides only the force necessary to meet and neutralize the danger. It does not have to expand into vengefulness that seeks to destroy, out of the fear that next time the adult may be successful. Adolescents know they can manage their own lives and do not need to destroy the competition. It is precisely because early adolescents are sure they could not beat their parents in a head-to-head struggle that their anger is so intense. Frustration is certain, and nobody likes that. But this anger serves a good purpose, providing the necessary power for the adolescent to feel justified in rebelling, even though the strength to win that war will not be available for a few years yet.

Most people who get into chronological adulthood feeling regularly slothful or vengeful (they make up the bulk of the workload of psychotherapists) have not yet learned how to be angry successfully. They either fall into overkill, and are wiped out by the retaliation or immobilized by the guilt; or they are frightened into slothfulness, believing that if they showed their anger, the indispensable people in their lives would withdraw their approval.

If you sense that you are angry more often than you want to be, and that your anger doesn't get you what you think it should, and if your life is more turbulent than seems necessary, you probably have fallen into the sin of vengefulness.

The prescription for that sin is to learn to be angry successfully: so that your anger can be pitched to meet the level of the other person's power, and can make it clear that you don't intend to have your freedom or safety tampered with, but also can make it clear that you do not intend to tamper with that person's. When that is achieved, your anger can become a tool for the resolution of conflict, rather than the kerosene poured on the fire. When it is applied as fuel to the fire, it perpetuates a chaotic and dangerous cycle of retaliations upon retaliations.

Vengeful people actually believe that if they abandoned overkill and were merely as angry as the situation required, if they stood face-to-face with the adversary in an open and angry examination of the merits of the case, they would surely lose. That being the case, they know they had better not do it, so they accelerate their vengefulness to drive the other person out of the arena, so that no such face-to-face exploration of ways to settle this conflict can be achieved. Your problem, then, if you are a vengeful person, is to determine what makes you so sure you would lose if it came down to a situation without intimidation. Since a great deal of my work is involved with people in just this situation, I have heard many reasons: "I've always lost before," "He'd find out I'm no good," "I'd find out I'm no good," "I'd look stupid," "I wouldn't know what to do," and many others. You can look at each of these fears on its own merits, and test whether you need to give in to it. If you don't know what to do, you can discover that you don't have to know what to do in order to do something. Knowing it in advance is not a luxury that anybody else in the human race has, so you aren't different and deficient because you don't know either. This can be a lengthy and painstaking process, but once people discover that they don't necessarily have to lose if they take the other on in an even match, they often stop trying to run the other out of the ball game.

Once that is accomplished, anger can be an asset and an aid to love, rather than an instrument of hate. If I can angrily let you know that what you are doing to the relationship between us is painful to me, that I won't allow it to continue without complaining bitterly, you are going to hear that much more quickly, and feel its importance more keenly, than if I let you know about it in a bland way which concealed the fact that it was important to me. My anger becomes a source of information for both of us concerning the importance of what we are about. It is not vengeful, does not seek to harm either of us, but can be quite loud, quite firm, quite insistent on changing the conditions that gave rise to it. If you feel the same freedom, and your anger can be a source of information and correction for me, then we have a relationship that stands an excellent chance of surviving for a lifetime and being a source of strength and love for both of us and those who come after.

This is a very difficult and complex skill to learn and is made more difficult and complex by the fact that it is new to most of us. We seem to be moving out of a societal era in which the hierarchical structures of "king of the castle" were seen as the only normal ones, and into a period in which equality among people is seen as more possible and desirable. Most of us know much better how to be either king or slave, child or adolescent, and are just beginning to perfect the behaviors that would be truly adult. But this growing knowledge of equality is crucial for the management of anger, because the anger of the slothful slave quickly becomes vengeful and often produces a total loss of safety for both slave and master; and because the anger of the king was vengeful from the beginning and—though simple to administer—it guarantees both rebellion and unfreedom.

# 5. Lust — Sexual Problems

Just like anger, sexual longing begins early, but genital fulfillment doesn't start before adolescence, and the ability of sex to dominate our personality is also an adolescent event. Physical maturity in size and sexual development, together with adolescent anger and passion, fuels the pressure for individuation and independence that marks the beginning of our insistent push for adulthood. Were we not coming sexually alive at that point in our lives, it would be a lot easier to remain older children in our parents' homes.

We have, of course, begun to see ourselves as sexual beings much earlier; and we have developed sexual role behavior and sex-linked skills. We have also learned the way the sexes relate in our families and in the institutions we frequent, and so have begun to sense what adult sexuality is like and what we will try to make it like for ourselves. So we arrive in adolescence with a fairly well established, if not strongly felt, view of maleness and femaleness.

Into these preexisting but not well-tested circuits adolescence unleashes an immense charge of hormonal voltage. For those of us whose fall into sloth did not postpone individuation far beyond biological adolescence, and for those whose choice of gluttony was not so powerful and visible that it took us out of sexual competition, that hormonal charge catapults us into an inner world that feels radically different, equipping us with bodies that are suddenly new and strange. For most of us, there follows a year or two of trying to figure out the internal changes, and of establishing ourselves firmly with same-sex friends. Once those tasks are accomplished, the highly charged, intense, and almost desperate struggle to figure out what to do with the opposite sex begins.

For those most limited and frightened (those swallowed up in sloth or gluttony), it does not begin at all—at least not until the sloth and gluttony have been overcome. For another group, somewhat less crippled but still desperately hungry for the appearance of an intense relationship that cannot be had at home, it begins early and with power. These are the almost-men and barely-women who are sexually active in their early teens, angrily and needily trying to reap a harvest not yet ripened from sexual play. Anger, pride, and a loneliness that knows no other solution are as often the powers behind this compulsive and semisexual coming together, finding frustration, shifting partners, and coming together again. Though sexual longing is one of the active elements here, it is only a small part of the mix.

Those who are a little luckier delay sexual experiments until they have learned something about relating to opposite-sex people, which usually doesn't happen until middle adolescence. It is hideously awkward at first, desperately important, exhilarating if successful and crushing if not. For almost all of us it has been our very most important priority for large chunks of our lives. If we have been lucky enough so that our sexual careers began on the ripe side of fifteen, it is probable that our first serious physical touching with opposite-sex youngsters that we were learning to care about and relate to happened over the next couple of years. It is a strange mixture of idealistic devotion, mortal fear, testing one's own strength, pushing the other's limits, learning how to form a relationship that matters, and exulting in physical touching of increasing intensity.

This distinction between early adolescent and middle adolescent sexuality is of crucial importance in the discussion of lust. The demanding, frightened, still basically same-sex oriented thirteen-year-old boy may be capable of erection and orgasm, but he is almost never capable of the complex give-and-take that is required to sustain a relationship for more than a few weeks. He must learn that, as must his twelve-year-old female counterpart. That learning comes through their having powerful yearnings toward one another and trying to do something useful with them. But what they do with them at those ages rarely can hope to take the humanness of the other young person very seriously. The inescapable self-preoccupation, fear, doubt, and embarrassment are, for the moment, too great.

One hopes that when those same youngsters are eighteen and seventeen—or even a couple of years earlier—they will have learned enough about who they are as individuals that they can reveal it to someone else; and being curious about the individuality of that other, they can begin linking their sexual longings with the capacity for love. Though at least in middle-class American culture they are far too young to be economically or emotionally prepared for marriage (and are even more decidedly unprepared for child-raising), they are beginning to be capable of the level of intimacy and caring that transforms raw sexual need into the poignancy and beauty of sexual love.

This brings us to the crucial and very difficult problem of defining lust. As with anger, it is clear that the physical emotion of sexual arousal is not identical with the sin of lust. In and of itself, sexual arousal is a God-given gift, joyous, attractive, bonding, and energizing. It is only when sexual arousal is combined with inattention to the welfare of the other that we have the sin of lust. Lust is here defined as that sin which occurs when we couple sexual longing toward another person with the willingness to place our sexual pleasure higher in our priorities than the well-being of the other, in such a way that the other and, thereby, we ourselves are harmed.

In my definition I have deliberately excluded any sexual act or motive in which there is no other. There has been a great deal written in every epoch of Christian history about the sins of masturbation, some of it partaking of the pre-twentieth century absurdity that masturbation makes you insane; some of it, more recently, consisting of more modest but still negative statements that ultimately masturbation ends in solitude and thus makes you lonely. These later statements often have the tone that suggests that sexual orgasm in the absence of a loved partner leads one away from the likelihood of ever having such a partner.

We now know that simply is not true, unless a person's own fears, guilt, and shame make it true. People who are not paralyzed by another sin (usually a crippling sloth that weakens all reaching out or the anger that leaves no other person acceptable) will simply not choose the pleasant rewards of masturbation over the more pleasant ones with a loved partner. This is one of those places where the free market works better than regulation. As long as sex between a man and a woman feels better than masturbation most of the time, people who have an option will choose it. The implication of the more severe critics is that a person can get so addicted to masturbation that he or she will not make the risky step of trying live partners. That makes it sound as though intercourse is like taking distasteful medicine, rather than being something capable of inspiring attraction that can get people to try to move mountains. For some few people it is that distasteful, but they are so frightened and slothful that they would avoid sex with or without masturbation.

We know now that most adults carry on parallel sexual lives, one masturbatory and one with a partner or partners, and that these typically overlap and enrich each other. The most difficult situations are those where people have been told their masturbation is evil, damages their relationships, and should have stopped long ago. Those people often worry enough about masturbation that the prophecy comes true. Thinking they have done damage to their relationships, they pull back, worry, and do end up with enough pain to inhibit relating. That can best be solved by attending to their fear about masturbation, not the masturbation itself.

Though we have become a sexually verbose society, one in which we see sexual stimulus almost anywhere we open our eyes, we are only beginning to believe that sex is good. Clearly our theologians believe it, most of the writers believe it, but our Sunday school teachers were never sure. And our parents, if they thought anything about it at all, usually kept those thoughts a secret. What they didn't keep a secret was their wrath and fear whenever our sexuality began to show itself, and so the message was communicated, often without intention, that sex is both dangerous and suspect, even if it is a lot of fun. But we are discovering, largely through the work of our sex researchers and students of personality, that the specific physical and mental results of sexual arousal and sexual gratification are almost completely and unambiguously good. Our muscles relax, we get exercise, our creativity soars, we feel closer to God and the creation, our relationship with the partner is strengthened, and we generally feel free to redirect attention to other productive pursuits (that attention having previously been contingent on finding a sexual release or controlling the wish for one).

So the problem does not come from the sexual arousal itself; in fact, it is possible that more good things have been done for the sake of sexual arousal than for any other human motivation. The problem comes from what does or does not go along with that arousal. There surely are situations in which the arousal, in combination with other motives, does do damage and is sinful.

At least five of these situations can be specified and their dangers explored.

1. *The Sick or Pregnant Encounter.* In the era before contraception and antibiotics it was much easier to say clearly that all nonmarital sex was sin. As the line from *Carousel* goes, "It's him that has the fun, my dear, and you that has the baby." The baby, and presumably the mother, suffers. The father escapes, sometimes paying a token cost but rarely participating fully in the burdens the shared act has created. There is no question that this was a sinful situation, and remains so today, if no responsibility is taken to prevent such an outcome. There may be no greater or longer-lasting damage a human being can do than allowing the conception and birth of an unwanted child. The consequences of such an act reverberate through the generations and probably never end. But in this day and time anyone who claims to have become a parent accidentally is doing at least a bit of self-deception, or the person's luck is phenomenally bad.

There is a special case of this kind of situation that should be examined briefly. There are a large number of sexually active young women, mainly in early and middle teens, who have access to birth control information but refuse either to protect themselves contraceptively or to avoid sexual contact. These girls want babies, and want them out of wedlock, in hopes of having something alive that is really theirs and that can give back love to fill the emptiness they feel. Their sin, though grievous, is not lust, for sexual desire scarcely enters the picture. Their partner's guilt is harder to specify, though lust plays a role in it; but these men and boys are as often selected and pursued as they are the selectors and pursuers.

It looked for a few years as if we had the problem of venereal disease licked, but it does not look that way anymore. Despite the widespread and inexpensive availability of effective treatment, more people now have venereal disease than ever before. This is especially true among adolescents, and it seems to result from a combination of ignorance, shame, and indifference. To make oneself, and even more clearly to make another, vulnerable to syphilis, gonorrhea, or herpes is both lustful and dumb.

2. *The Exploitative Seduction.* There is a class of sexual encounter that is about as loving and concerned as is an eighth-grade boy twisting the arms of the girls in his class to show he is stronger than they are. The exploitative seduction tends to be derisive, sometimes intimidating, acquisitive, and generally not much fun for anybody. The motive of the perpetrator comes as much from gaining power, either over the partner or with his or her own peer group, as from sexual arousal and release. This particular ilk of sexual sin was once considered an almost exclusively male phenomenon, but one of the less happy results of women's liberation and the singles bars has been the growth of predation by females as well. "I can make you want me." Of course, this is not altogether new, though it is considerably bolder in the urban meat shops than it was in middle-class high schools and colleges a decade ago. At that point the competition for the promising and desirable men was carried on in less overt ways—though securing the handsome pre-med that all the girls in the sorority wanted may have had as much to do with the wish for sharing position and wealth as with any sense of the tenderness the two could share.

But the most painful examples of this category of human abuse continue to be the sexual harassments that are more the province of men than of women. Whenever a woman is placed in the position of having to accept more sexual contact with another than she wants, both lust and anger are involved and damage at some level is inevitable.

That leads me to a note on rape. Rape is almost never a crime of lust, but a crime of anger that uses sexuality as a weapon. It hovers somewhere at the very beginning of adolescent development, borrowing a great deal from the rage an unhappy adult has carried from the second or third year of life. As nearly as current research knows, the typical rapist is not triggered into action by the stimuli that arouse sexual longing in most people. The crime seems to be initiated by his perception of a vulnerability in the victim, and/ or a resemblance of the victim to another person he would like to harm and humiliate.

3. *The Subtle Perpetuation of Fruitless Patterns.* I worked recently with a very attractive woman of thirty-four who had been divorced in her early twenties and had lived alone for twelve years.. She liked men, enjoyed sex, and had gone through a string of lovers during those years with an increasing sense of sadness and futility at her inability to get anything strong established with a man. Her relationships would follow fairly similar patterns, with early meetings being warm, easy, somewhat exciting; first dates being fun and leading quickly to sexual sharing; and further movement toward exclusiveness of relationship going on without a hitch. But when commitments began to be talked about and futures entered the picture, things would go sour. She would leave, or he would leave, or they would both leave and come back, but none of these relationships would last beyond the first year. It was obvious that there were some basic relationship skills, typically learned in young adulthood, that Mary had not mastered. She had learned how to feel comfortable in herself with her sexuality, and she had learned how to establish a warm and enjoyable relationship with a man. She just hadn't learned how to move from the decision to be intimate exclusively with another to the ability to implement that decision. She was feeling the hopelessness of continuing to deal with men like this, which is what brought her to me for counseling.

Her story is by no means unusual. Though there are a number of men and women in the single life who want to remain single, most see it as a transitional step into an enduring monogamous relationship. But something fails to happen that would convert the often well developed relationship-getting ability of these people into relationship-keeping capacity that would undergird engagement and marriage.

For these young and not-so-young persons, lust has played an effective and cruel trick. They learn, often in middle adolescence, how to be gratifying and pleasant as companions and sexual partners. They expected that this skill would be all they would need to find enduring relationships. They stopped learning. Now each new relationship begins the same way the previous one did, the same moves are tried and succeed all too well, the familiar old road is followed again, and the new one which might go somewhere is never seen. To be the sexual other with such a person is to let one's arousal supersede both the partner's welfare and one's own. There comes a point in such a relationship when the sadness of knowing how the story ends comes close to the surface, and thoroughgoing honesty might lead these lovers to hold each other and weep over their inability to be what is needed for each other. To hold one another and make love, though it is pleasant and may be tender, often perpetuates the illusion that this by itself will be enough to sustain relationship. It would be far more loving now to let the consciousness of the bankruptcy come through, so that both could act on the certainty that this bartering in sexuality will never by itself produce the relationship that is wanted and needed.

It is not only unmarried lovers who are impoverished by this lustful situation. From time to time married couples appear for treatment with one or the other complaining that the party of the second part wants sex only once or twice a day. Since it is the only way one or both know to establish any sort of contact, almost any moment without it seems intolerably lonely. Sex becomes either a substitute for relationship or the only channel of relationship open to the pair.

This is terribly common, in a less exaggerated form. Because of its ability to produce immediate comfort, plus its being a symbol of committedness, it's easy for a married couple to use sex as an analgesic against all kinds of pain that need a more basic remedy. Hence lust—desire plus both indifference and fear—introduces lovemaking instead of deeper talking or another needed activity; and the pattern that needs correcting continues to erode the relationship.

4. *The Breaking of Contracts and the Creation of Trouble.* There are situations where our sexual urges create bona fide difficulties in our lives and those of the other, even when we are not being exploitative and even when we are not repeating neurotic patterns. The most obvious of these times are when one or both sexual partners are acting in violation of an established commitment to another. It is rare for adultery, within a traditional marriage, to escape being a source of guilt and withdrawal on the part of the adulterer—even when there is no discovery, mutual humiliation, or acknowledged betrayal. That is true regardless of the marital dissatisfaction that may have made adultery attractive in the first place.

There are other ways, too, by which the lure of lust builds major practical problems in our lives. How many women and men have had important efforts ruined by the embarrassment that comes from the discovery of a casual sexual encounter, not to mention those who have lost important time and failed in significant accomplishments because of an investment in sexual pleasure that does not lead beyond itself into relationship.

Part of the beautiful danger of sex is that it can blind us to awareness of whose interests need to be considered in our decision-making. In the moment of building desire, it is very easy to feel thoroughly justified by briefly considering the possible good or ill that can come to one's partner and one's self; but by doing so one may place in jeopardy the well-being of others who have a claim on the loyalty, time, or productivity of oneself or one's partner. "Others" is by no means limited to spouses or children. It also includes those who have an investment in the effort that the time otherwise would have produced or in the reputation, not otherwise vulnerable, of one of the partners.

5. *Routinization.* Perhaps the most common way in which lust is the preferred sin for respectable people is in their allowing sexual experience to become so habitual, so uninvested in the other as the unique person he or she is at this moment, that it ceases to carry the freeing and often saving power that good sex can have. Routine bears with it a number of evils, first of which is the gradual deadening of the ability to respond in the area of life that can keep us most powerfully alive. If we allow our primary sexual relationship to become dull and give us nothing, but continue to engage in it to gratify only the physical hungers, we are well on the way to a death of spirit that can be irredeemable. A divorced woman once said to me of her former husband, "He said we should keep doing it because it was good for us, even if we didn't like each other."

It is surely good for us, but not when taken like bitter medicine. Perhaps lust is no more involved than sloth in such death of the soul, but the failure to at least signal the poverty of the relationship by refusing the act allows the perpetuation of the fiction that life is being shared in a vital way. Better than this is either no sex at all, or the end of that relationship so that something else can begin.

One question becomes clearer as our discussion proceeds. Is sexual desire, in and of itself, ever sufficient grounds to conclude that the sin of lust is being committed? The answer is no! Lust is the combination of three necessary elements: (1) sexual desire; (2) action, either physical or fantasied, which attempts to gratify that desire; and (3) indifference to the well-being of the other.

As with the other sins, a physical reaction or an emotion

cannot in itself be sin. An intention is required, and the intention must include the absence of active caring for the other and the relationship between self and other. It is not possible to categorize situations according to their external characteristics, such as married or not married; but it is possible to categorize them according to these internal characteristics.

In this situation the sexual desire increases the potential for damage from other possible sources of harm, such as sadism or ignorance. It is like the gun in an armed robbery; it makes the consequences of the act more dangerous to both its object and its perpetrator. Sexual interest makes us more vulnerable because it is so important. Our defenses are lower, and personal slights or abuses are accepted that would otherwise be noticed and opposed. The vulnerability we place ourselves in when sexually alive puts a higher requirement on our partners for consideration and mutuality than do our more protected ways of sharing.

The crux of this, especially for married lovers, is our indifference to those aspects of the other that don't enhance our sexual goal. The other person's fatigue or fear or need to be known in nonsexual ways is so much easier to ignore in seeking the habitual and dependable comforting that comes from sexual release.

It is a bitter irony that the same capacity that can give us the most intense pleasure can be counterfeited in a way that lets it offer only the disappointment of finding that our connectedness with the other was an illusion. It arouses the greatest hopes, hopes that reach deep into an unconscious that remembers physical touch as the sign of ultimate trustworthiness. But because it arouses such hopes and has the power to gratify them, it also incurs the obligation of a clarity that makes it nearly impossible to misunderstand its intentions. Sex that is discovered to be only self-gratification is the bitterest of insults and betrayals to the lover who received it as a full gift of self.

Our expectations of what is good and bad in sex, beautiful and dangerous, have a major self-fulfilling quality about them. The woman who believes that her husband could not possibly love her if he had sex with another woman is going to be damaged in a very different way from the woman who believes that such adultery, discreetly and on occasion, is an acceptable if unfortunate necessity for marriage. The question of which one is right is not of as much interest to me as the certainty of the power that the expectations hold. It was once possible to say, in the realm of sexual behavior, that certain acts with certain persons meant specific things about the loyalties, allegiances, and meanings of the participants. Not too many years ago it was said with confidence that there were two kinds of women, wives and whores. Whores enjoyed sex, and nice girls, whom you would marry, didn't. Hence, if a girl enjoyed sex, she was not a good marriage candidate. That expectation had a great deal of power, regardless of the fact that it probably wasn't true then and certainly isn't true now. Consider the adultery of a husband whose wife believes that such an act necessarily shatters the fabric of a marriage: it is a more serious sin than the adultery of a husband who has a certain understanding about such things with his wife. The difference is in the extent of the pain and humiliation for her, and in his willingness to inflict it. That is not to say that other kinds of damage, perhaps more subtle, that adultery creates would also be less in this kind of consensus situation, but only that there is a difference in the pain.

The same is true of the belief that there are only two kinds of women. If everybody around you believes that, and you are known to enjoy sex, you have cut your chances for a conventional family life in later years. If you are a woman who enjoys sex in a situation where people don't believe that sexual activity makes you unfit for marriage, then it may be that your enjoyment improves your chances for an enjoyable family relationship in later years. In the first situation, to be openly sexually active may be lustful sin, because it endangers much of what you would otherwise be able to create with the rest of your life.

One of the things that we need to look at is whether the sin in that situation is entirely the responsibility of the woman who indulges her sexual appetites, or if some of it isn't better seen as the fault of a society that creates attitudes whereby sex is seen as ruining the potential for future relationships.

I am not suggesting that anything people say is O.K., is O.K. There are certainly some sexual behaviors and attitudes that are more damaging and/or more creative than others. I am saying that the data are not all in, but that some acts we formerly thought were always wrong are clearly sometimes right.

In a situation like this, where the boundaries between damaging lust and potentially beautiful sexual desire are so unclear, how does one know if one in fact is in lust, and in need of repentance, forgiveness, and change?

In many cases it may not be possible to know until after the fact (by their fruits you shall know them). But in many situations there will be obvious indicators. Though it doesn't end the discussion, the question, "Who can be hurt?" must open it. If there is a person whose legitimate interests would be damaged, to proceed toward a sexual encounter is sinful.

Unfortunately, the answers to that question themselves are typically ambiguous. Many people think they have legitimate interests in other people's sexual behavior, when in fact they may not. The divorced or estranged spouse in a marriage that has shown all signs of death may not have any appropriate input to the question of the former partner's sexual behavior. The person may be hurt, may feel saddened or angered or outraged by it, but to honor that feeling would be to sanction slavery. Also, parents of grown children often feel a definite interest in regulating their offspring's sexual behavior. At some point (but which one?) that interest ceases to be legitimate. Is it at age fifteen, eighteen, twenty-one, forty? Those questions have not been finally answered, but anyone who pursues a sexual relationship with a person in that situation must be prepared with some answer.

There are also situations in which you may want to claim that no one has a legitimate interest in your sexual decisions, when they in fact do. "What she doesn't know won't hurt her" is one such example. There is no way of being certain she won't know; and it's even more likely that the changes in you, because you know, will be felt by her even if she can't identify exactly how things aren't the way they're supposed to be.

Though it probably is not often true that parents have a legitimate interest in controlling the sexual behavior of their grown children, it is more often accurate to say that children growing up have a real stake in the sexual behavior of their parents. They have a right to a stable environment in which they feel cared about and secure. A parent's sexual behavior can jeopardize that. Growing children have a right to learn about sex as a joyous experience that increases the richness of life, a right not to be saddled with a belief that sex is unimportant or dirty on the one hand, or hazardous and unmanageable on the other. How a parent handles his or her sexual feelings will have a major impact on how that comes out. Children have a right to see that your living by your principles, sexually and otherwise, makes you happy— so they'll have hope in following your example. And they have a right to be presented an image they can respect, which first means a pattern of behavior you can respect and that is not too widely out of step with the community's practices. At times that may require restraint when otherwise it wouldn't be necessary, and at times it may demand the courage to take risks. This is a solution we must seek both for ourselves and for those for whom we are ultimately responsible, our children. If your own life is not sexually enjoyable, and if you yourself are preoccupied with lust, you are very likely not equipping those you are raising to avoid this problem in their maturity. And since this problem is so universal in our society, it won't be totally solved by any one of us in our own lifetime. The most we can do is to make the best contribution we can to our children's ability to live well.

But if by acting on sexual longing you will damage yourself or your partner by perpetuating a routine, damaging other more important aims, or deepening a pattern that is dangerous to intimacy, then lust is afoot.

Unfortunately, such determinations are difficult to make. So we probably have to rely on questions like "Who can be hurt?" Only rarely will our sexual situations be confidently disposed of by answers established here or elsewhere. There remains one crucial and ultimately reliable question: "Is your sexual behavior enriching your life?" If it is constantly getting you in trouble, or if it is rarely providing fulfillment and joy, then you are damaging your chances for fulfillment (and God's joy in you) in some way that can only be sinful.

If you decide that this is the case, what should you do? There is not a lot to be gained by the self-conscious and vigorous attempt to avoid lusting. If that were effective, you probably wouldn't have been lusting now or would have fallen into some difficulties more grievous than those which lust has introduced you to. A single-minded attempt to avoid lust can only occupy more and more of your total mental effort, leaving less and less energy free for the living of life. In this sense, the old adage that the quickest way to be rid of temptation is to yield to it has a certain ironic and valuable truth. But that does not mean that acquiescence to our established habits is the holiest of courses. To do that would be to consign ourselves to continued nonfulfillment and potentially destructive relationships that gained us the label "sinner" in the first place.

No, the alternative is not to negate the negative. The alternative is to refocus one's attempts to find out what is interfering with the positive ability to develop real, enduring, enjoyable sexual love. It is the development of such relationships, in which sexual desire is invested in other persons who themselves are rich with meanings for the self, which provides the best possible immunization against lust.

The basic strategies for diminishing lust's control over your life vary, depending on whether you are or are not part of a well-invested and enduring sexual relationship. Let us first look at the case of the single person who is not currently in a promising relationship. The first question is, Why aren't you? Is it your greater commitment to sloth, to anger, to gluttony? How do you regularly attempt to engage people? Or not to engage them? If you don't know, you'd better find out. Look in the mirror; ask your friends, especially those of the opposite sex who don't seem to be interested in you; if that fails, I would suggest a talk with someone who is professionally charged with knowing about how people engage one another: a pastor, a pastoral counselor, a psychotherapist. If you do not identify the ways in which you fail to seek and win the commitment and affection of opposite-sex people, you will not stop lusting.

Now let's look at strategies for people who are in long-term committed relationships. Here we find two kinds of obstacles to sexual fulfillment that open the doors for lustful sin. One is the explicitly sexual, and one is everything else. There are, in turn, two kinds of particular sexual difficulties that can mess things up even for a once-good sexual relationship. One is that it can be overtaken in the competition for time and space with the other involvements of life. Children, job, church activities, and all kinds of ostensibly good things can so crowd in on a couple's time together that sex gets crowded out of the central role that it must have to provide immunization against lust. A couple who are having trouble getting this done need to leave their children at somebody's mother's and get out of town for a few days by themselves, seek out some deliberately sexually stimulating situations to prime the habit-encrusted pump, and commit themselves to some mutual enjoyment. If that doesn't seem possible or desirable, it's usually a sign that something else is wrong with the relationship.

The other possibility is that one of the partners has become so inattentive to his or her own, or the other's, sexual attractiveness that the biological and aesthetic stimulus that arouses the physical fires of sexual longing has been swamped under too many whiskers, too much fat, too many flannel nightgowns, too much booze, too few showers. It is the responsibility of a person who wishes continued sexual investment from another to continue to make it possible by not killing the excitement. We know a good deal about how people of any age can keep in shape, can manage weight, can affect the structure of their bodies; and we have always known about how people can be made to look attractive by good grooming and attention to dress. The husband who complains that his wife is never sexually interested, but who himself has gained fifty pounds since the marriage and rarely takes a bath, has some responsibility for his having a lot of lustful fantasies and for his difficulty in keeping his hands off his secretary—who probably can't afford to push him away since she is dependent on him for her job.

Any couple that can't resolve their lack of mutual sexual excitement by the combined use of these two methods is probably masking some significant relationship difficulties that are causing their lack of sexual excitement. It is very difficult to be sexually aroused toward somebody you don't like or toward somebody with whom you are currently or chronically angry. There is nothing that will make that sexual situation significantly and lastingly better until the relationship stresses are remedied. That demands some serious talking about what is the matter between you and your partner, and staying with that until some data are produced that lead in the direction of resolution. Again, if no data are produced—or if they are produced but lead only to bickering and fighting that does not bring about creative change —then I would recommend that you bring a third party into the situation, one who can help you identify the ways the two of you are killing each other's ardor.

If you don't remove these obstacles to sexual fulfillment in your relationships, I can practically guarantee you that lust will be a constant companion; and the odds are pretty good that it will break through in behavior that causes trouble for you and the others you care about.

Now a bit more about children, who often come into adulthood so damaged in their sexual attitudes that lust-immunizing fulfillment is never possible. The most important thing parents can do to immunize their children against lust is to show them by example and precept that sex, in the context of their relationship, is fun, valuable, and helps them be together and invest in the life they all share. The fact that mommy and daddy like to touch each other, and value time together which the children are not invited to share, is one of the most reassuring things that ever happens for children. It is the single most important thing that the parents can do; to such an extent that if they do that well and consistently, there may be no way they can fail.

But there are some additional things that you as a parent can do, or refrain from doing, that will make a continued difference. One of those is to be as permitting and comfortable toward your child's inevitable masturbation as you can bring yourself to be. For some of us that requires stifling a well-entrenched preference that our children not embarrass us, but it is quite important that children be allowed and encouraged to explore and enjoy their own bodies. I do think it's important that children learn that there are places where that is and is not appropriate. You would no more want them fondling themselves in front of your guests in the

living room than you'd want your guests to watch you and
your spouse making love. But the question there is the time
and the place, not the inherent goodness or evil of the
activity.

Another principle that I would suggest is that the transition between a sexually naive and quiescent childhood and
a sexually active postadolescent adulthood should be as
gradual and as relaxed as possible. If the first possible messages about sex come to a woman the night before she is
married, it can be practically assured that it will be years
before she can guiltlessly enjoy her own sexuality and that
of her spouse. If she is regularly getting signals in early and
middle childhood, early and middle adolescence, that sexual contact is enjoyable and good under the proper circumstances, it is natural that she would look forward to sexual
relating in adulthood as a source of gratification and goodness.

A client of mine recalled how her good Pentecostal
mother had told her over and over as a young girl that she
should always be careful not to be an occasion of sin for a
young man. That meant that she was not to be attractive,
that she was to dress very conservatively, that she was to
limit severely the amount of touching that could be allowed
between her and a date, and that she should convey the
impression of being neither very interested in nor very interesting for sex. That same person came to me after marriage, reporting that her mother had also said she knew it
was kind of peculiar to expect that sex would then be all
right after marriage, but "that's just the way things are."
What I'm saying here is, that's not the way things are. Inevitably sex will seem as virtuous and valuable in our children's
twenties as it did in their teens. If we wish to free them from
a lifetime of struggling with lust, let us free them now from
the dangerous blockages that will impede a joyous mature
sexual relationship.

To say the same thing slightly differently: The most lusting and the most dangerous lusting is done by people who are sexually unfulfilled, not by those who are sexually overgratified. Gratification, if it is real, reduces appetite and preoccupation, not the contrary. Most of us lust far more vigorously, and with less concern about the consequences, before we have figured out a way to develop relationships that will give our sexuality a happy and productive outlet. If we don't do too much damage, we can learn a lot from whatever lust we get involved in. The irony is that if we are too preoccupied with avoiding the lust, we are likely not to do the learning, and thereby likely to fail to become mature enough to make the lusting unnecessary.

Our society and our church have rightly identified faithful, monogamous marriage as the most gratifying and sacred of sexual expressions. They have often failed to see that monogamous marriage is a goal that cannot always be reached by excluding all other kinds of sexual learnings. It is the very rare person who is so well equipped by childhood that he or she can move from complete sexual naiveté into engagement and marriage and have the sexual aspects of those relationships work. If we want a large portion of our society to reach the goal of a faithful, adult marital relationship, we may have to be at least understanding toward the inevitable lustful behavior people go through as they develop ways of reaching that objective.

If you do reach the point in life where you are ready to commit yourself sexually to another person, having both the powers of decision and the technical skills to make the relationship work, and if you have taken seriously the questions about your commitment to productive sexuality that we discussed earlier in the chapter, then there are some rewards you can reasonably expect. You can expect that during the greater part of your adult life you will have gratifying, flexible, strong, and sexually powerful relationships, in which your sexual passions and possibilities can be fulfilled as vigorously as there is energy for. You can also expect that you will have—as a bonus for not having spent overmuch energy attempting to get such a relationship established or fighting the lust that may have urged you to seek a less acceptable outlet—a great deal more energy for the living of your life. You will begin to experience your sexual desire in much the same way as you experience your desires for food and rest, as something that has its own rhythm, that can be satisfied without bending everything else out of shape, and that can be a source of dependable and life-enriching satisfaction. That in turn will give you confidence in yourself as a sexual person with the capacity to give and receive pleasure in this most powerful of ways. As a direct consequence of those rewards, you will have much less likelihood of damaging yourself and other people through behavior inspired by the sin of lust.

# PART IV

# The Sins of Exaggerated Adulthood

---

# 6. Avarice—Greed

Though the fundamental possibility of all sin is laid down in infancy, there are some sins it is almost impossible to develop fully until we have adult powers. These sins develop from the natural capacities of maturity; the ability to accumulate possessions, the realistic wish for a place of honor and respect, and the achievement of inner integrity and self-confidence. Though a person is working toward these objectives from birth, they are rarely achieved in their fullness before middle age; and the sins they stimulate flourish at the times in life when success is most available and its absence is most galling. Avarice, envy, and pride are the sins of the prime of life.

"Avarice" is the sin of loving the act and the state of possessing, more than one loves God and his creation. Not that it is sinful to love things. It isn't. But it does warp and impoverish life and mar a person's relations with one's fellows to love the having and controlling of things. Martin Buber's magnificent description of the relationship between a man and a particularly fully seen tree in *I and Thou* demonstrates that it is no sin to stand in awe and humility before some object that God has created. But it is a loss to us, and a rip in the social fabric of the cosmos, if we become so intent upon our exclusive having of that thing that the beauty of the object and the pleasure it can bring are insignificant in comparison to the issue of whose it is.

The ability to be avaricious dawns before we ever go to school. Anyone who has watched the tantrum-ridden struggles of two three-year-olds over the one shovel in a sandbox has seen its beginnings in action. Though children must learn about possessions and boundaries in childhood if they are to manage property as adults, all of us seem to step quickly beyond the necessities of owning, and move into the needless and false identification of our very selves with that which we can hold in our hands. Eric Berne has observed that "Mine is bigger than yours" is the first of the intimacy-robbing games that humans learn to play. Even the young child tries to water down the uncertainty he feels about his own competence and lovability by asserting the superiority of what he owns.

We also learn early to substitute the giving and receiving of objects—often a direct invitation to avarice—for more reliable tokens that we are loved and the promise that we will be protected. Probably few parents for example, returning from a business trip or second honeymoon, have escaped the typical reunion scene at airport or garage door, punctuated by childish cries of "What did you bring me, Daddy?" In my household those words have often preceded "Hello, how are you? I'm glad you're home."

This is nearly a universal sin in the worlds of those who write and read books in the United States. Middle-class Americans are taught from very early that it is of immense social importance to own certain objects. The objects differ from time to time and from region to region, but the failure to comply meant that you simply didn't have access to the people of interest and importance in your community. In my own childhood, after the coaxial cable reached Kansas City, the key object was a television set. In practically everyone's adolescence now, it appears to be an automobile. For some of my clients who entered the social whirl in the last decade, it was Bass Weejuns and Pendleton sweaters. Today it's more apt to be central air conditioning, three-piece suits, and Chemlawn. The social penalties for failing to place the ownership of these objects ahead of other priorities (including, especially, our judgment as to the worth of the objects, which is by definition irrelevant), may be the exclusion from desirable, life-fulfilling communities and relationships. Most of us don't have the strength of character and creative relationship skills to escape this demand that we place such selective avarice at a high point in our value structures.

Avarice is often thought of as a particularly American, particularly secular sin. It is not lost on many of us that the economic health of our society seems built on our willingness to spend every possible hour of our day making every possible dime we can make, so that we can spend it on every possible good that can be advertised and marketed, so that our neighbors who advertise and market these goods can have incomes. At times it appears to be important for us to spend even more than we have, so that the assembly lines will not stop running, and to be sure to buy that which our neighbor has made rather than something that might have been more carefully manufactured by someone else's neighbor. And what we buy, we must preserve.

The ancient fable of the ant and the grasshopper (in which the former saves but the latter sings—and later goes hungry) gives strong cultural sanction to the personal habits that often lapse into avarice without our being aware of it. Though the stockpiling the fable endorses is not strictly for its own sake (the coming of winter requires it), the dividing line between industry and thrift, on the one hand, and a graspingness that seeks accumulation for its own sake, on the other, is often and easily missed. How do we decide how much is enough to preserve us from expectable crises like winters? How do we decide how much protection is reasonable or sinless in a world in which the majority have no way of protecting themselves? Surely the attempt to eliminate more than our fair share of that risk inevitably leaves us in avarice. But how much is fair?

The story reveals another dangerous thing about the diligent accumulation of wealth. Though the fable doesn't suggest that the lot of the ant is an unhappy one, in popular imagination it's only the grasshopper who is having any fun. The accumulation of goods can become a joyless, mechanical function, in which the relationship between the possessor and the coveted object is stripped of all its aesthetic and utilitarian elements. The object can become only a characterless marker in the ant's game, contrasted with the apparent joy of the grasshopper's consumption. One might come away from this story preferring the grasshopper's ability to allow his objects to produce the pleasure they were created for.

The social pressure to possess objects that in many cases we wouldn't need or want for themselves makes this a particularly complicated problem. In many cases these objects are symbols indicating that we have made it to a certain level of accomplishment and wish to be seen as having achieved that which we truly have achieved. One of the rewards for such achievement is the companionship of other achieving people, so we are in an actual bind when it appears we may be deprived of that status, and the fellowship that goes with it, if we do not choose to make or spend money in ways deemed important by people whose friends we would like to be.

In the long run this difficulty complicates identifying avarice when it is present; and it also points out how our slothful willingness to let other people determine what is right for our lives appears in the guise of the sin of avarice. If our failing is passive compliance, we will suffer in the more muted style of sloth rather than through the keen pangs of avarice.

But we wouldn't make objects into idols, or the owning of objects into a standard of admission to polite society, if the ownership of some objects wasn't pleasant in itself.

There are very many things that it is more pleasant to own than not to own, ranging from elegant, warm, comfortable homes through the finest gourmet foods and down to the simplest and most unlovely pile of gravel—if you happen to need gravel.

Some objects we have to own to be safe—or think we do: locks on doors, roofs on houses, brakes on automobiles or bicycles. Some objects we must have to sustain health: medicine, adequate and well-balanced meals, furnaces in our buildings, quiet places to sleep. Other objects are necessary to win us inclusion in friendships and love relationships: It's hard to play tennis with a friend if you don't have a racquet, and even more difficult to spend an evening with your beloved if you've fallen ill from malnutrition. And we're accustomed to thinking of humanity's fullest development as closely tied to objects: how can you play Beethoven's Appassionata Sonata without a piano, or write a poem without a pen and paper? Comfort, aesthetic excellence, the passing of time with friends, safety, health, all demand the ownership and control of some objects.

God commanded Adam to have dominion over the earth, and we have only implemented that command with special zeal by our proliferation of goods and our dedication to having them. There is nothing evil about that, far from it. Precisely because it is necessary for life and pleasurable, it carries the potential for being loved too well and sought to the exclusion of experiences of even greater value. It feels good to have things when we want them, so it is not unnatural for us to fall into the belief that to have more is always better. But—as I have found with my cooking—the axiom "If one clove of garlic is good, three must be better" isn't true. It also isn't true that struggling to own two of something when one would do is a fruitful way of investing our lives. Such a belief is not fruitful for us, and often is devastatingly destructive to others.

This leads to an important special case of avarice, plus a

whole range of marginal situations we need to examine. The special case is our frequent intent to possess something that by its nature cannot be possessed. The attempt to own another human being, either through the formal institution of slavery or through the inappropriate excesses of power that often go with employment, political loyalty, and family oppressiveness, is the first instance of this kind of avaricious sinfulness.

But there is a wide field of improper ownership, the precise extent of which can't be determined without deciding what is appropriately ownable by a human being. This differs from society to society, and some of the great disputes of human history have centered around this question. Exploitation of the Native Americans centered largely around the issue of whether land could be privately owned. In Anglo-European values it clearly could, in tribal values it clearly couldn't, and the support of values that in our society aren't considered sinful led this nation to slaughter them. Who decides? Marxists, either by formal political ideology or by private persuasion, tell capitalists that the ownership of the means of production by private individuals is immoral and dangerous. Some Marxists would kill to preserve what they see as the right of the worker to own the means of production, and many capitalists would typically kill to preserve what they see as the right of the entrepreneur to maintain ownership. Which one is avaricious? The same dispute is currently raging at another level between the environmentalists in this country and the advocates of free exploitation of energy. Who owns the earth? Who has the right to decide how much control can be exercised by the person who has paid the money and been designated the possessor of certain objects?

We cannot know the answers to these questions, and it would probably be foolish to assume that whatever answers do exist remain the same from year to year. But in our attempts to own whatever in God's eyes is unownable we are stuck in our sin, with the risk of destroying both ourselves and the object for which we strive.

That gets further complicated when we look at the whole range of marginal cases. How do we decide whether it is avaricious for 5 percent of the world's people (Americans) to consume 35 percent of its resources? Does individual motivation around that consumption even matter, when it approaches the point where my wanting a sirloin steak for dinner means that so much grain is fed to a steer that not enough is left for you to have a piece of bread? In our decision whether to call my behavior avaricious or not, does it make any difference whether I want that sirloin steak out of an inordinate desire to possess, or simply because I have a keen aesthetic sensitivity to the qualities of fine beef?

These questions point us to the issue of national avarice, group avarice. We often catch ourselves when we would overstep our neighbor's rights—for example, to get just the television set we want—and we have the chance to change our mind and repair the damage. But what hope do we have of knowing the infinite number of situations where the organization of the world is such that we get bananas or pineapples from the fields that tropical subsistence farmers need to grow grains or vegetables to keep their families alive? The complexity of the world means that hardly any American, no matter how low on this society's totem pole, can take a bite of food or put on a piece of clothing without participating in the exploitation of someone else here or abroad. Our avarice is organized so well that we don't even have to know we are acting on avarice when it is getting us what we want.

What to do? Even while we are organizing to get ourselves more information and undo the most hideous of the evils, we eat the bread and drink the cup that the world economy has strong-armed from our neighbor. There is no freedom from this sin, even if your individual heart is pure. Your government, your grocery store, and even your school system, has implicated you by the services it offers and the prices it charges. Repentance and humility, coupled with an effort we know cannot cleanse us, are our only proper responses.

John Ruskin wrote, over a century ago, that the act of keeping yourself rich is also the act of keeping your neighbor poor. As we know today, that statement is too general to be universally true, but we must suspect that it is true much of the time. Though we are inescapably compromised on the national and international levels, as individuals it may make a difference how one becomes rich and goes about remaining rich. One of the more or less inescapable rewards for a productively lived life in a capitalist society is money. For many people it is almost impossible not to make money if you're doing things that are really useful and you don't deliberately turn it away. This statement may be more true for some people than for others in the society; but in general it is more true than not—even for people not invited into the center of the money economy, once they learn how the system operates. It is certainly not evil to have money, or property, or power; nor is it automatically virtuous to be poor. Some people are poor because they have been systematically excluded, on the basis of their racial or family background, from learning how to get money; other people are poor because they don't do very much to prevent the condition. But much of what can be done to prevent poverty is a well-kept secret in some parts of the society. Many well-educated middle-class white Americans would find it hard to become poor if they wanted to, but the things they know about how to get money are not well known in the ghettos (of many racial and religious groups), in the mountains, in many of the rural areas, or even among persons as close to centers of power as most American women. And people have kept the knowledge of those methods to themselves in a way that can only be described as avaricious, teaching huge masses of our population to remain in their place—be that the home, the factory, the menial jobs, the other side of the tracks—and by systematically denying them the formal and informal education that would equip them to compete with an equal chance of success.

This is not to deny that there are ways of becoming wealthy that are a genuine and immense boon to those who are not wealthy. Surely some wealth is an appropriate reward for achievements such as the creation of the automobile, the writing of a series of fine plays, or the successful distribution of services that had not previously been available to people. And few would object to the notion that the investment of the industrialist really does produce a substantial real benefit to the people he or she employs. Wealth itself does not convict of avarice, but the restriction of the capacity to become wealthy to certain groups should be enough to produce an indictment of those groups. There are real differences between the various possible ways of becoming and remaining rich. The businessman who works diligently to preserve his wealth by opposing all possible social services to those who can't afford to provide them for themselves is closer to avarice than the one who regularly gives away a large proportion of his income. The businesswoman whose management of an industrial concern is marked by her suppression of any attempt at the development of representation for workers is different, when it comes to avarice, from the one who implements an effective means of participatory management. These are not simple questions. Sometimes the difference between one of these ways of doing business and the other is the impracticality of extending decision-making authority to people without the information to make decisions. But sometimes the issue is the avaricious enjoyment of controlling the lives and destinies of other human beings as though they were chattel.

Yet we must remember that it is not evil to be competent, and therefore well paid, and that it may well be destructive to be so preoccupied with the apparent well-being of the downtrodden that one forgets the managerial necessities that enable the survival of a business or of a society. Ignorance—when entrenched in positions of power—can be as destructive as raw evil, and it can rarely be maintained without the help of some sin, usually sloth or pride.

This is why avarice is an unmistakably adult sin. To be effectively avaricious one must have the skill that is a prerequisite for acquiring possessions. What produces the sin is the temptation to so seek the having that one forgets both the limits of one's actual needs and how one's having affects the life of one's neighbor. The only way to know whether a particular act is avaricious is to look closely at the treatment of persons and other unownables in the creation of wealth and in its use. It is of course wrong for any group to monopolize the power, and hence the choice, to give or not give. But the only group who can give much materially, who can contribute much to the ongoing welfare of a people, are those who have much—whether the much be in money, property, or power. So the dispensing of effective mercy is dependent on the prior accumulation of resources. It is the failure to use wealth productively, the preference for holding it and gloating over the control it gives one, that marks the sin.

A continuing question in this book concerns the valuable objective the sinner is pursuing when he or she falls into a given sin. There is always something sought that is worth having, and that situation is true for avarice as well.

Its objectives are different at a person's different levels of growth. In childhood, avarice is usually a way to reassure oneself of the love and investment of a much-needed parent. A little later, avarice is an attempt to get and hold on to something that is dependable in the face of a world that continues to change. In young adulthood it becomes a matter of making our mark competitively: "Life is a game and money is the way you keep score." It feeds then on the fact that the world rewards successful performance with a supply of goods and services. By middle age our avarice capitalizes on the thoroughly appropriate wish to provide for old age and leave something for the children. All of these in and of themselves are worthy objectives, but all are very near the borderline of exploitation and destructiveness.

Awareness of these things forces us back onto the question, "How much elimination of the uncertainties of life can we strive for without falling into sin?" We all want to be safe. Yet to attempt to protect ourselves too vigorously, to make protection too central to our attention, quickly blinds us to the need of and for our brothers and sisters and encourages us to believe that our security comes from a source that cannot in fact provide it. Further, those drives can kill our ability to appreciate the object in itself, as an entity that has an existence and qualities to be enjoyed apart from the question of its ownership.

One of the tangible damages done by avarice is that of preventing us from fully loving the object which we own, from really gaining as much from it as it has to offer us. The more intense our avarice, the more zealously we will protect the object that we seek or own from the possibility of being touched, harmed, damaged, or enjoyed by other people. Aside from what this does to our human relationships, obviously the effort interferes with our freedom to enjoy the object itself. How fully can we enjoy an object that we must keep hidden even from ourselves and under lock and key, as contrasted to an object that we may view through a pane of glass—even an object that belongs to someone else? The use, hence the enjoyment, of most objects tends to change them, even to wear them out and render them less and less things that can be owned, or valuable to own. So to keep them, we avoid enjoying them. There are times when this situation is true of money, so that it can be more avaricious to hold on to it, and keep it safe, than to invest it and run the risk that it may be lost. Witness the parable of the talents, in which the one who was accused is not the one who profited, but the one who merely maintained his master's goods. To give an object its proper dignity and place in the world is to have an active relationship with it, to do something with it, and that something may involve diminishing or transforming its continued value. But the avaricious man or woman can be so bound by the need to continue to own the same object tomorrow that the ability to use and enjoy it today is lost.

Another tangible damage done by avarice comes from its demand that the thing desired, and with it all of the universe that impinges on that thing, remain static. This is the flip side of the loss chronicled above, but it carries the added pain of obstructing the ongoingness of life. If I trust and love the world, which is another way of trusting and loving God, I must also be willing to submit myself to the reality that all things change. But if my investedness is in owning things, it is also inevitable that I will want those things to maintain the value and the substance which they had at the time I gained possession of them. Since nothing does that, in reality, I am forced into an increasingly defensive and ultimately impossible attempt to turn back the inevitable changes that time itself produces. As the Scripture reads, "Moth and rust corrupt." As inflation is teaching us, even money decays. When we invest ourselves in the attempt to keep something as it has always been, so that our ownership of it will matter, we are placed in opposition to the natural flow of the world.

There is a further brokenness we actively create. When I am concerned with my ownership of things, and you either want or need those same things, we are inevitably in conflict. We then make it difficult for ourselves to know and value anything of each other except our conflictedness. The signs of this damage are easily seen. The constant struggle in our cities between those who anxiously own the goods of this society and those who desperately would like to own them is an almost daily reminder. An expansion of that same observation brings us to an awareness of the struggles of nationalist and liberation groups throughout the world against those they see as avariciously hoarding the goods of their societies. Our current struggle about whether we will have petroleum and at what cost is a direct result of the conflict that follows avarice.

But we need not look so far away. When my colleague and I want the same raise and the resources will allow it to only one of us, there is usually a link between my zeal and the damage I do to our relationship. Many organizations are severely weakened by leadership being more concerned about the money they can make right now than about the long-range welfare of the group.

All of these are active ways in which this particular human failing damages our lives. Beyond these sins of commission, avarice can lead us to a particularly chilling sin of omission. We not only break our human fellowship with the have-nots when we actively snatch away the last crust of bread, we also allow it to diminish when our attention remains fixed on what we have. We become merciless without active intent, merely by continuing to devote our attention to having and getting, and failing to see the plight of those with whom we share the world.

I have heard it said that a person born to wealth in this country can easily go months at a time without having a two-minute conversation with anyone whose income is below the national average. Even if we are persons of moderate income, we are so typically surrounded by others who share our style of life, and have interests, views, and resources like our own, that it is difficult for us to be keenly aware that there are some whose very survival is a matter of constant struggle. That is one reason why it is easier for a camel to pass through the eye of a needle than for a rich person to enter the Kingdom of God. Special effort is required, an effort not providing immediate reward, if persons who are accustomed to wealth are to become conscious of the needs of those who are accustomed to desperate struggle. It matters little that one's appearance of indifference is due to lack of information about the plight of those who suffer, since our lives are often limited by dozens of infinitesimal avaricious decisions that serve to keep us unaware. The damage on both sides is deep. Actively seeking knowledge of those who need our mercy is a prerequisite for staying out of avarice.

But we know we cannot avoid all sins, and we cannot avoid this one. All of us at times fall into avarice, and some of us have specialized in it. For those who have found themselves most clearly described in these past few pages, what can they do? What is the remedy for a life that has become habituated to avarice?

Often you will hear Christians saying that the cure for avarice lies in Jesus' statement to the rich young ruler, "Go, sell all you have, give the proceeds to the poor, and come, follow me." But Jesus did not mean that as a remedy, but rather as a sign by which this man could tell whether the remedy had come. To sell all would not undo the avarice, though if the man were no longer avaricious, he might be willing to sell. Jesus was asking the man to demonstrate that he was ready for fellowship with God, not describing the best way to get there. Possibly it would be easier for the rich to escape avarice if they first became poor, for then they might discover that it is possible to be poor and still find life valuable. But many have made that transition only to find that poverty increases avarice, and they have struggled all the more viciously to become rich again. The remedy lies instead in learning and coming to grips with what one is trying to create or to avoid by owning everything in sight. Without that, poverty is merely an inducement to more desperate possessing, as sexual deprivation is a stimulus to lust.

A realistic first step is to clearly identify what we are trying to possess and to decide whether that thing is really possessable. Then we can decide what possessing it is expected to accomplish for us. If we have been truly avaricious, we will almost always find that we are trying to accomplish something that is not in fact accomplishable or is not worth as much as what we sacrificed in the attempt. We must be clear about what it is we really want, and about the actual value to us of having it, if we are to move beyond this sin and escape its effects. Seeking poverty won't help, since both you and I can be as avaricious about our right to own a matchstick as we can about our desire to own an empire. We must come to a decision about whether our aim is worth accomplishing, and by what terms. If we find out that our aim is not worth accomplishing, then our curiosity must increase even further. What motive bound us to the illusion that it was? Or if our aim is worth accomplishing, can a way be found to reach the same end without such greed?

Often a way can be found to accomplish one's aims without avarice, but it usually requires a willingness to share the control of one's destiny. If I own something myself, I am safe; but if I share the ownership with you, then my safety is dependent on the relationship between us. It is so much simpler not to be vulnerable, not to have to consider whether I can relate to you in such a way that you will choose not to thwart me. How else can I be safe? The answer is that there may be no way to be safe, since in fact the safety in this method is illusory as well. In my avaricious attempt to be safe, I inevitably produce enemies who may heartily enjoy preventing me from reaching my goal, or dealing me the blow I most fear. How much more vital, how much more joyous, to place my investment and my confidence in the ability to build a relationship—one in which you will want to cooperate with me in using our shared resources to minimize my danger, and yours as well. This may require a great deal of flexibility from me, but in its pursuit I will be alive and involved with the world and its creatures, and I will produce no less safety for myself than

I would have with my grasping.

In fact, many of us have been taught that we need far more safety than we do. We've been taught to seek safety in that which can be kept. And we do so, largely because we distrust our ability to diminish the other's wish to attack by our own loving and lovable behavior. In most avarice there is a powerful kernel of self-doubt, leaving us trusting only what we can get from the things we possess. That seems far more dependable than what we can bring about through our own humanness. So often the accomplishable part of what avarice seeks to produce cannot be achieved by avarice —but it can be achieved by developing our ability to get people to want to love us and to help us when we're in trouble. Our need to own the whole world decreases as we increase in confidence that someone whom we don't own will want to come to our rescue. But to reach that goal we have to become more committed to and more skilled at the things that encourage other people to want to respond to us.

In the last analysis, though, perfect pleasure, perfect enjoyment, perfect safety, perfect supremacy, cannot be achieved. No matter what we own, we will die. No matter how high we rise, we (or our descendants) will eventually fall. Much avarice is the attempt to deny this undeniable fact, and to bemuse ourselves with counting our possessions rather than face the frightening reality that ultimately we or those we love will be defenseless—if not at the hands of the world, at the hands of our own aging and decay. Ultimately, the only immunization against the avarice that attempts to prevent such loss comes from the faith that the world and its processes, both those of advancement and those of decline, are in the hands of a force that ultimately wills, and will preserve, our good. Perhaps only that can transform the unacceptable, which we will always try to defend ourselves against with some sin, into a reality which we can embrace with hope.

# 7. Envy—Jealousy

Envy has a bad press. The classic commentators find less to say in its behalf than for lust, avarice, or any other sin. If the books are to be believed, it is that rarity in human experience: something that almost everybody does, almost all the time, but that never feels good to anybody. Yet there must be reasons, however hard to find, for its almost universal attraction.

"Envy" is the sin of wishing that evil might befall someone else who has something I want, so that I, instead, might get it. It is the sin of wishing to prevent someone from achieving the good fortune I think should be mine. Envy also applies if the thing longed for is mine, but I suspect that you will try to get it, and I wish you damaged. It is wishing that you not be in the place or position that you are, because I want it for myself and fear that you will keep me from having it.

Unlike avarice, the sin of envy is a uniquely personal sin. It is not concerned with my wanting the thing that divides us, but rather with my attitude toward you, my real or potential competitor. Envy is my quiet satisfaction that you don't have what I have; it is my longing that you might get your comeuppance; it is the blind wish that you might not have any happiness that I cannot reach; it is the fearful demand that nothing which might jeopardize my superiority over you be allowed; it is the prerational lashing out against every real or imagined threat to that which is most precious to me.

Envy springs from my conviction that there is something I must have, or be, or accomplish. That conviction is more powerful than my simple wish to have that status, but it contains the driving demand that if I do not have it, I have failed in a hideously shameful way, carrying a punishment I cannot afford to take. In the presence of that demanding necessity, most of which I place upon myself, I see you as either preventing me from having it or reminding me, by your success, that I don't have it. I am hopeless in my belief that I cannot achieve it through my efforts, so I invest my energy in building a fantasy or creating a reality in which you are deprived of that which reminds me of my failure.

Anything can be the occasion for envy. In earliest childhood we envy our parents and our siblings for the closeness that they seem to have with each other, at those moments when we want it but can't seem to get it. A little later we envy the toys or pets or clothing of other children. As adolescents we resent the athletic prowess or physical beauty of those we compete with. But it is in adulthood, especially around the age of forty, when we develop the greatest expertise at this peculiarly divisive human failing. By this time it is becoming increasingly clear which of us in any given generation are most likely to write the finest plays, build the biggest fortunes, win the highest offices, and raise the brightest children. It is no longer easy to believe that I can have these things I've longed for by merely redoubling my efforts. I begin to stare directly at the possibility that another—a rival, perhaps, or even a friend—will permanently have more of what I want than I will have. It is then that the temptation to hate the other is acute, and anything the person is or does or has can remind me that I feel I have the right to occupy the place that person has. It is especially galling—and more so the more enviously unhappy I am— if the other is happy. Then any trifling event in which I see the calm or peace or pleasure of the other can stir up a storm in my soul.

Envy comes in a number of discernible varieties. The classic form is the have-not's envy of the have, as typified in Marlowe's famous epigram, "I cannot read, and wish all books were burnt." It is probably the easiest kind to identify, and the most persistent in our consciousness. It is seen in the wish of a client who woke up every morning struggling desperately with her fears of everything from being alone to being in a large crowd, and who told me ashamedly one day how much she hated me for seeming to be so calm, for not having anything obvious to suffer over. The pain in that woman—struggling with knowing she needed me in order to have hope for her own future, yet tormented by my visible reminder of her own failures—is a standard for envy.

It shows us something of the divisiveness, the isolating effect of this subtype of the sin. In many sins we can at least let the rawness of our evil be seen and it will be appreciated somewhere: the object of avarice or lust is often at least flattered by the intensity of our wish, the cook is joined with us in an appreciation of our gluttony; but in only very rare moments can we bring the envier in us into the company of the envied and not expect a righteous rebuke.

Aristotle's knowledge of this variety of envy showed in his statement that envy grows most naturally in a society of equals. We are taught to believe that we start even. So if we look around and find that we are not ahead of others or even with them, we feel our failure keenly because we have also been taught that we should finish first. If we don't finish first, we are less than we ought to be; and to accept that is to be seen as weak. The more thoroughly we have been taught, the more likely we are to feel outdone if the next person has more of anything or is better at anything than we are, even if there are as many or even more categories in which our accomplishments and accumulations are greater. Democratic ideology can breed a belief that the only way I can be your equal, which I am supposed to be, is to be identical—to have everything in the same measure that you do. Since this is impossible in a finite world where some of us have developed expertise and interests different than what others have, the inevitable pain of envy toward those who have more of an attribute, a possession, a skill, a state of mind, or a reputation daily increases its contribution to our sense of having been cheated.

There is another kind of envy. It belongs to people who are actually rich in resources, but who have convinced themselves that they are poor. This is doubly hard to stamp out because the feelings of envy are based on an illusion, so it is difficult simply to appeal to obvious facts of the world. All envy requires some illusion. The belief that I cannot achieve an enjoyable life while lacking any one of life's goods is always false. But this envy requires that illusion plus the additional one that I am actually deficient in the commodity in question. This is the envy of the beautiful woman who thinks herself ugly, toward those who are merely attractive; the envy of the well-liked man who thinks himself unpopular, toward those who are merely tolerated; the envy of the great athlete who thinks himself barely adequate, toward those who would be overjoyed to come close to his performance. In many ways it is like the envy of the have-nots for the haves, for that is what the envier believes it to be. But it is even more confusing, even more isolating, because the rest of the world sees the ugliness of the envy but fails to see what can possibly be causing it.

This envy develops from a lifelong habit of expecting betrayal and abandonment. For example, it comes from a woman's knowing, before any data are available, that "my beloved will always prefer the beauty, the wit, or the mere availability of any possible competitor; despite whatever she or I may do." The result is an escalation of fear and anger that cannot be stopped by input from the real world, because such input is systematically reworked to fit the belief that "I will again be chosen against." This feeling can produce such desperation that intensely dangerous and destructive acts can seem to be the only effective way of preventing the threatened loss.

I know a man who utterly cannot bear for his wife to take a call from a lifelong woman friend. The panic sets in, confirming his belief that nobody could really love him, and that anyone, especially his wife, would invariably choose the company and attention of anyone to avoid being with him. The desperation reaches such a point that only a violent explosion in the marriage blows off enough steam so that things level off again. The pain of this brand of envy is heightened by the fact that this man well knows he may lose his marriage because of this furor of distrust.

Then there is the envy of the have toward the have-not who may supplant him. This is similar to the previous type, but differs in being based on the actual reality that all possession, all position, is temporary; and that each thing that is gained will eventually be lost, and we know it. It is a backhanded envy, subtly withholding respect from anyone approaching peership with the envier. This is the feeling that impels the teacher to make it very clear that even his brightest pupil is not quite his equal. It is the feeling that individual staff members in a successful agency have that guarantees they will make sure any questioner knows the difference in quality between them and their nearest competitor. It is the subtle sadism, the comfortable superiority, that makes it obvious the envier is more interested in being seen as number one than she is in maintaining the excellence that earns that rank.

This form of envy doesn't produce the bitter, obvious explosiveness that comes from envy based on an illusory deficiency. It is a subtler, secret vice that waits not quite calmly beneath the veneer of apparent satisfaction in having achieved a position. It is only when someone else threatens to do nearly as well, raising a question in at least the envier's mind about who is really number one, that the uneasiness and anxiety become obvious. Though some of us have become skilled at hinting about our competitors' shortcomings in a way that masks our fear of their getting something that rightfully belongs to us, it is difficult for any of us who have done well to glowingly praise anyone who attempts to stake out some of the same territory as our own. And it is even more difficult not to be a bit too pleased when some shameful discovery is made about this competitor, or when his most productive staff person suddenly leaves him for greener pasture. Then it is only with a substantial infusion of the grace of God that I can be in full fellowship with him at the next professional meeting.

How do we get into these disheartening predicaments? What desirable thing could we be trying to accomplish that leaves us so isolated and ashamed before our friends?

Some of the things that stimulate us to envy are very natural and require no special gifts to understand. When we are very young, totally dependent on the goodwill and competence of our parents for our very survival, and on their tenderness and love for our growth in self-esteem and hope, we become envious when we see their attentions and loyalty being devoted to another person. Often that person is our other parent, who always seems to come between us and the one we desire just when we are about to get enough of that life-giving contact so that we will never have to worry again. But that other person is four times our size, and obviously secure in his or her right to be as close or closer to the one we want than we can possibly be. What can one do but envy?

We are too small to fight, and even if we weren't, we would need that so-and-so to help bring home the bacon or fry it up. Furthermore, if we did succeed in fighting off the other person, there would be very nasty consequences from the very beloved we are fighting for. Some of us, instead of experiencing this first with a parent, make the same galling discoveries in relation to a more powerful older sibling or a more winsome younger one. And again, despite our most fervent efforts, it is all but impossible for us to out-muscle big brother or to out-need baby sister. And even if we could, there would be retribution from parents who seem not to understand how desperately we want what the other seems to have.

So we move into fantasy. We imagine, in our envy, that one day daddy just doesn't come home from work; or that mommy does in fact run off with the milkman; or that little brother has an unfortunate accident at the baby-sitter's. And in those fantasies our envy is rewarded, contrary to the beliefs of most writers on this sin. What can be as gratifying as those secret, private moments in which the other who stands in our way is obliterated, shamed, or defeated, and the field is left open to us? There may not be one iota of reality in those stories, but for a few seconds inside our heads they can make us feel as secure and hopeful for life as we would ever want to be. Who could wish for a greater reward?

Though we learn to envy at three or four, or even sooner, with skillful parenting we may realize we won't die if daddy or little sister gets the lion's share of mommy's love, and that we can do some things that will change our seemingly helpless and hopeless position. We may realize that we can grow into the kind of person that mommy would want, and we hope that somebody quite like mommy will choose us a few years down the road. After a brief experimentation with envy, if we are among the fortunate ones, we will turn our attention to more productive real-life efforts to get the rewards we seek. If we do that, even though we have developed a very strong streak of envy as a way of coping with the great powerlessness of childhood, and even though we'll never be completely without situations that prod us to feel that helplessness again, envy will not again demand to dominate our lives. In the meantime we'll pick up a lot of learnings (some highly questionable) about what a person must have and do for his or her life to merit respect. Depending upon who we are and how we are taught, the list will vary, but for many it is a list of intimidating length: beauty, wealth, power, a desirable mate, a respected profession, happy and achieving children, a lovely home, a powerful car—and the list goes on forever. The more things we add to our personal list during adolescence and young adulthood, the more vulnerable we are to later situations in which some of those necessities appear to be out of reach. The more powerless we feel to achieve them, and the more intensely we believe we must, the more certain we are to envy those who do.

As long as it is not yet clear what we can become, envy is not so great a danger. In most of adolescence and even young adulthood, we still have power over how we will stack up against our fellows. Obviously there are exceptions, and envy does thrive on the exceptions: a sixteen-year-old with one leg, or a five-year-old with leukemia, can hardly be expected to avoid occasional resentment of those who are luckier. As for most of the things we are anxious about when young, we would do better to be industrious about them, because we can still change them. But after a certain point in life that is no longer true, though the point does vary depending on the life. A working-class black woman who marries a truck driver at eighteen, not having finished high school and already with a baby to raise, may really be in a powerless position more incurable than that of a thirty-five-year-old white man who has just seen that the new appointee to the fourth vice-presidency in his company was thirty-three.

But for all of us there comes a time when it appears that our place in the pecking order has a solid upper limit, and at some later point that appearance proves true. Then the options can be grim, unless you are fortunate enough to have achieved the things on your personal list of necessities for an acceptable life. And even if you have achieved them, you remain vulnerable to the subtle approach of the envy of the have for the have-not.

But for the less accomplished those choices are often quite limited. Suppose you decide that you are never going to be what you have told yourself you must be to have your own respect, and thereby you suffer a crushing and possibly terminal blow to self-esteem; or alternatively, you may choose the occasional shadow triumphs of enviously and invisibly destroying the opposition and leaving yourself as the Queen of the May or King of the Hill. It may take only a few small doses of envy a day to undo the crushing weight of failure enough to want to see tomorrow.

After the first rush of envious triumph has passed, you are left with a numbness toward the parties you have envied and with your own presumed failure. In the numbness you can quickly forget the other's feared or hated accomplishments, your own vulnerability, and especially the self-administered shot of envy that dulled the pain. Depending on the magnitude of your failure, this fix may last anywhere from a few minutes to a few months. But, inevitably, if the pressures you put on yourself are real, and if the others (or even your own thoughts) are at all persistent, you (or they) will produce another stimulus, which will bring on another chilling awareness of possible failure, which will require another dose of envy to set the balance straight. If you are an accomplished envier, you can maintain this cycle with only a few fractions of full awareness at each transition, deftly employing the fantasized victory (the defeat for the other) to still your own doubts about yourself. It never lasts, but if you are alert enough to the dawning of awareness, a new dose can always be administered in time to prevent a crushing pain.

The failure of this system begins when you catch yourself at it, which is what the numbness is supposed to prevent. Someone looks at a man and says, "I believe you're jealous (ha ha)," but he's not laughing. Or he notices his embarrassingly conscious thoughts of the disaster he half hopes and half fears will befall his closest friend and competitor. Or he becomes aware that there are certain people toward whom he feels particularly dead, despite the fact that his widely known empathy and understanding are available to practically everyone else. Or possibly he reads a chapter like this, and begins to notice himself in the numbness, in the bittersweet half-victory, and in the embarrassment most of all.

So what's the harm? Does this repeated venture into self-narcosis damage anything? Or is it just a tasteless, but only embarrassing, instance of poor form?

That question can be asked without embarrassment because the effects of envy, though powerful and destructive, are also much more subtle and hard to see than those of gluttony, lust, or anger. It would be easy to believe there are none, but that would be false. "Envy maketh hard the heart," and that is its greatest destruction. It proceeds by building a dependence on the ability to make oneself numb by once again fantasizing the defeat of the enemy. Like any satisfaction, it reinforces, becoming more and more available as the source of comfort the self needs to survive. Since this satisfaction depends on the twin conditions of believing that you have been cheated and imagining yourself avenged on the cheater, the world increasingly is seen in adversary terms. That has two further effects, blindness and loneliness.

The more one envies, the less one sees oneself. The actual treasures and accomplishments of one's own life become as nothing when the attention goes to what the other has and is. If you have been taught that your only salvation is in intellectual brilliance, and you are constantly being reminded of the superior brilliance of someone with whom your daily life is shared, whatever other fine qualities you may have will be neither seen nor enjoyed. That is at least an aesthetic loss of real importance; but it also produces the tangible effect that you misjudge yourself, thereby constantly putting yourself into situations that are not fitting, and avoiding situations that would be.

I know a young woman who learned in early childhood that teaching was the one way she could do something worthwhile, molding young lives and performing a service for the community. That propelled her through high school and the early years of college at a high rate of achievement, but when student teaching came along she found her classroom to be a combination of baby-sitting and riot control, saw her supervising teacher so underpaid it was embarrassing, and felt no respect from either teachers or administrators at the school where she served. She abandoned her wish to teach and went into private business, where she regularly saw people advanced or hired in her corporation not on merit, but because they knew somebody. She became preoccupied with the real and imagined rewards others gained at her expense, today seeing herself as having been a fool and having no skills worth marketing. The envy so distracts her that she routinely avoids situations in which her substantial business ability and sharp mind could bring profit and esteem. Her envy against those who have gained positions she felt they did not deserve has completely blinded her to the actual, if different, paths to a socially productive career and a decent income for herself.

But if envy promotes blindness to self, it is even more disruptive of the ability to see the other. When life is going well, awareness of other people provides us with our greatest source of learning and some of our most dependable pleasure. Watching or listening to a person who incarnates the best of humanity or who has perfected a desired skill is for most of us a high point of life. But for the envious it cannot be, for the pleasure is overwhelmed by the regret that one's own skill or personhood is at a lower level. The more envious one is, the fewer performances in art, athletics, design, or anywhere else can be an unambiguous source of pleasure. The pleasure always struggles against jealousy, which dulls the joy and secretly carries the wish that the other be less than perfect.

Joy is lost in the inability to view the other's excellence, but there is also loss in the failure to see the other's weakness. To the envious, the one envied is always larger than life, dangerous, unreachable, invulnerable. But no one can actually be so, hence the sinner has overestimated the danger and underestimated the potential in relating to the envied other. For example, when I see the other as a person who has no needs, then I forgo the opportunity to be the meeter of his or her need. If my colleague is seen as having more of commodity X or reputation Y than I have, I may fail to note that in relationship Z I am her equal. This damages my self-esteem, makes it unlikely that I will hear her cry to me, and perpetuates my need to use the only weapon I have.

In not seeing my colleague clearly, I will miss her reaching out; and in fervently imputing weakness to her for my self-esteem's sake, I will miss her admission of actual weakness stemming from her striving to grow. The chance that we might have a reconciled relationship diminishes, and the danger of actual damage between us from one to the other expands.

This leads to the deepest wound envy leaves, the absence of relationship. Whatever part of your being wishes my ill and hides the wish from me is out of relationship with me. Nothing that either of us can do will bring us into full human contact until that wishing and the hiding of it are given up. The more envious you are, the more your relationships are illusion and pretense. The more people surround you, the more alienated and alone you are. Each person is a potential threat, a reminder of your failure, providing an occasion to exercise your envy and return to the numbness that the contact weakened. It is hard under these conditions to deliver the bread of life to your neighbor, for the neighbor will see it as a vain attempt to demonstrate the skill of your baking.

Both existing present relationships and possible new ones are stunted by the sin of envy. A man I once treated went into every social situation, whether it was a poker game or a sales meeting, frightened that he would perform poorly, angrily envious that one of his colleagues might perform well and make him look bad by comparison. Other men in those groups thought they were his friends, but he could receive nothing. Only one thing frightened him more than being with those who thought they were friends, and that was to be alone with the self he knew was an enemy. His self could do nothing well enough to guarantee safety against a humiliation that would not end.

As envy is one of the toughest sins to spot in another, and one of the easiest to hide in and from oneself, it is also one of the hardest to transcend. There is no way to avoid the opportunity for envy, unless you live in a vacuum and have no memory of the excellence of another. Praising the other will only produce the question of why no one praises you. And if the impulse to envy is there, restraining it on one occasion will give it redoubled energy for the next.

But there are things we can do to diminish the power of envy in our world and in ourselves. I'll start with the things we can do for our children and those parts of ourselves that are still children, in hopes that the damage is superficial enough that we can heal it by conscious effort.

The most important single prerequisite for envy is the belief that there is something I must do or have or be to be acceptable, primarily to myself and secondarily to the world. As parents it is frighteningly easy for us to teach that belief to our children, and as adults it is terribly difficult for us to stop believing it. But when we catch ourselves believing it, or when we catch ourselves believing that there is something our children must do, we have spotted an idol we are worshiping in envy. An acquaintance of mine is fond of saying, especially to his children, "There is no substitute for achievement." When his children find they cannot achieve in some arena, they fall ill; when he makes the same discovery, he questions the point of remaining alive. When either is confronted by the tangible accomplishments of another, the feeling of envy is crippling. When we find ourselves in this position, we must ask ourselves whether, in the absence of a given achievement (or whatever we lack), life is worth living. We could phrase it differently: "Are any of the other goods of life of any value for us now?" The answer is almost always yes, though the next person can see that more easily than we can.

That question often brings another awareness, one that may not be so easily confronted in the conscious mind, and that therefore may require psychotherapeutic investigation. To say that something else is of value is often to directly contradict the wishes and values of a parental figure we can scarcely afford to alienate. But this idolatry too must be examined, so we can be free to decide for ourselves whether our lives are acceptable. If we establish our own criteria, looking inward at what we value and believe, we are in a much freer position from which to admire and enjoy the other person, as well as the creation and its Lord. First we must discover our own beliefs about what makes life worth living. Otherwise we will continue to blame someone else for our failure to get whatever it is we lack.

There is a second order of prevention, typically the appropriate means for children and adolescents. For most of us, in our early life our possibilities are much vaster than we imagine, and to some extent that is true until we die. But it is especially typical of youth to see differences in accomplishment as differences in substance, when they are really differences in experience and training. If we are in envy at those points of life, or if we notice ourselves encouraging those in our care to see differences in substance at those points, we are encouraging investment in fantasized victories rather than in efforts toward real accomplishment. Anytime we catch ourselves believing that some particular success of our neighbor is beyond our own possibilities, we need to look very carefully at the process by which we came to that decision. We must constantly ask ourselves whether there are any data proving that our best efforts would be in vain. Many times envy of this sort stems from a defeatism that has based itself on an envy-determined, weak picture of ourselves, one that fails to do justice to the potential for increase in capacity and in accomplishment. When we catch ourselves believing that it can't be done, and that we may as well take solace by undoing the doer, we need to ask, "Who told us it couldn't be done, and what evidence did they present?" If the evidence is based on anything less than our best and most liberated efforts, our decision to stop trying and start envying is needless and reversible.

This is another of those situations where our view of reality is often skewed by our allegiance to that reality's interpreter. Many of us have been told over and over again by our parents that we couldn't do this or that crucial thing in life, and that we'd better believe what they say. When we find ourselves believing in our incapacity for reasons like these, it is time to look closely at whether we can afford to remain so dangerously loyal to the worst in these loved ones.

In any adult situation where we find ourselves in envy, we must first submit the envy to the two challenges described above, namely: "What do we believe makes life worth living?" and "What evidence is there that we can't succeed?" But there will be times when those will be answered and the envy still remain. That's true because much of our envy stems from a self-rejection more basic than the lack of any specific skill and more far-reaching than the failure to achieve a particular goal. Some of us could not name the success we would have to achieve to be able to love ourselves. And until we do that, we will not be able to stop wishing destruction on the neighbor for reminding us that we do not measure up. When we catch ourselves in that predicament, we must recognize that the neighbor is an innocent bystander in a sadistic game we ultimately play against ourselves. If there is nothing that I can do, no single accomplishment that would bring me self-acceptance, then there is nothing that the envied neighbor could refrain from doing long enough to give me the power to love myself. It is so much easier to blame the neighbor and then to destroy that person in fantasy, than to see the void in myself and rage against my self and those who helped to leave it empty. But to see things as they are is the only remedy. Only when I discover myself believing that my predicament would be better if my neighbor's were worse (so that I can then confront that belief and recant it), only then am I on my way to triumphing over the envy within me.

Overcoming envy will ultimately require at least two confrontations beyond our facing this mistaken belief. First, we must deal with those persons in our past who left us believing that nothing we can do will be enough. Secondly, we must come to terms with the God who, despite our sinful doubts, accepts our insufficiencies and is able to remedy them. In the last analysis even our self-loathing is an act of envy, for it demands that we not be simply as we are. To be as we are is to accept the fact that our insufficiencies, even our failures, are part of what we have been given by One who loves us, and that we are therefore worthy of our love as well.

# 8. Pride—Conceit

Shelley's poem "Ozymandias" describes a desert scene through the eyes of a traveler.

> Two vast and trunkless legs of stone
> Stand in the desert . . . Near them, on the sand,
> Half sunk, a shattered visage lies, whose frown,
> And wrinkled lip, and sneer of cold command,
> Tell that its sculptor well those passions read
> Which yet survive, stamped on these lifeless things,
> The hand that mocked them and the heart that fed:
> And on the pedestal these words appear:
> "My name is Ozymandias, king of kings:
> Look on my works, ye Mighty, and despair!"
> Nothing beside remains. Round the decay
> Of that colossal wreck, boundless and bare,
> The lone and level sands stretch far away.[4]

The sin of Ozymandias is pride, that exaltation of self which believes no one else has anything to say that the prideful woman or man needs to hear, but that every word from those lips merits the attention of all.

Pride is often called the first of sins, and it is treated at the beginning of most books on this subject. The classic position has been that humanity's prideful refusal to accept the authority of God, and thus to place itself at God's command, is a necessary forerunner of all the other sins. The tradition has held not only that pride goes before a fall, but that it is pride that acts as the detonator, the release mechanism, for all other innate vulnerabilities. They would otherwise be contained and limited by our alliance with the power and love of God. But when pride declares superiority to the need for that alliance, tradition tells us that those innate weaknesses are released and given power to complete our separation from God in the other six deadly ways.

What, precisely, is this most powerful of sins? It has been variously described as "inordinate self-esteem," as having too much love for self, or thinking too highly of some specific accomplishment. It is termed "the sin of the first person singular," the attempt to appropriate the perfection of God, and the belief that one can save oneself.

Some of these traditional wordings must be discarded or modified in response to new knowledge developing within the psychoanalytic movement. Unless the words are being defined in a most unusual way, it is simply not possible to love oneself too much (one may, of course, love others insufficiently). We have learned in the last ten years (primarily through the work of Heinz Kohut) that it is when we have failed to learn to love ourselves in early life that we inevitably and destructively try—and fail—to make up for it in adulthood. But what we give ourselves in that attempt to catch up is not love, but a desperate, intense self-preoccupation that has little in common with the gentle, forgiving, growth-producing attitude we usually call by that name. When the self's hunger for affirmation and acceptance is satisfied, there is an automatic withdrawal of energy from the struggle to get love and a resulting calmness and peace that provides the only effective basis for the ability to love another. I can no more love myself too much than I can put too much water in a glass; the excess simply runs over the top. On the other hand, it is possible for me to worship myself overmuch, to attribute a significance to myself that far exceeds what is real, but that is not love. It is more accurately a kind of self-hate that has to deny what I really am by claiming to be something more, saying indirectly that the actual self I am is unacceptable.

The same disclaimer is appropriate to the idea of having too much self-esteem, though the issue is somewhat less easy to define. Self-esteem is that feeling toward oneself that puts one forward (not above). It is the reward of believing that, despite my flaws, even my sin, I am lovable and capable and can expect this to be confirmed by most of those with whom I come in contact; that I have the right to hold up my head in the company of other human beings, who also have the right to hold up their heads; and that I stand before God as much in need of grace as any other person—no more and no less. How can one believe too firmly that one is a full human being? It is this belief that frees persons to risk, to create, and to love—knowing that even if the effort fails, we cannot fall beyond this basic foundation of human dignity.

Then there is the idea of having too high an estimation of the quality of an achievement or performance. This is a different matter, since what is at stake is not the worth of the person but the quality of some event or artifact the person has had a part in. In certain areas, one performance may be objectively better or worse than another, which is never true of persons. A time of 9.5 in the hundred-yard dash is not as good a performance as a 9.2. The issue does get more muddled when one tries to say that one artistic or business accomplishment is better or worse than another, or when one tries to compare athletic teams from different sports or different seasons, but even then one could imagine setting up specific criteria which one or the other could more completely fulfill. There is a basis for deciding whether a given claim is inflated or not. Perhaps Muhammad Ali can rightly say, "I am the greatest" without sinful pride, if it is understood that he is talking about heavyweight boxers in his generation, and talking in terms of their athletic ability and accomplishments. It is equally true that almost anyone else who makes that claim about anything cannot do so without sinful pride. Obviously, in deciding whether that statement —even from Ali—is a prideful one, more is involved than simply asking whether it is accurate or not, but if we know it is not accurate, we can be almost certain it is prideful.

So I do have to concede that some instances of over-estimating the value and importance of a contribution are prideful, though it is pride in a small-scale way. It is a minor-league kind of pride, a pitiable step-sibling of the sin that rises to its most formidable power when the claims made by its author are accurate. Pride in a nonexistent or fatally flawed accomplishment is a delusion that can be destroyed by leading this second-class sinner to an accurate perspective on what she or he has done. This puffed-upness cannot be the heart of the most lethal of sins, since there is pride that cannot be reduced by accurate vision. It might be better said that this overestimation falls more at the overlap of envy, avarice, and gluttony than within the territory of pride itself.

The most dangerous pride comes when the claims of the prideful person are unmistakably true. The pride consists not in the magnitude of the claim, but in setting oneself apart as different in substance by means of the claim. There is a crucial difference between the accurate self-assessment of one's own excellent work and the pride that cuts one off from the other. The sin is in the belief that because of this excellent record my substance itself is superior, that it needs less to be under review, that it needs not to hear what the other says, that it is above reproach, above dialogue, above supervision, and above peership.

We should enjoy the excellence of our work and the exercise of our skill. But that enjoyment becomes destructive when the recognition it brings becomes more important than the excellence, and when we lose the connection between the two. Pridefulness is locked in when our fear of losing that recognition, which seems to set us apart from and above all others, leads us to resist letting anyone assess the presence or absence of the excellence.

It is the thanking God "that I am not like other people," the establishment of myself over and apart from them, which defines pride properly. It is placing myself above others and even potentially above God, clearly at least on a par with the divine. The traditional link between pride and height is precisely because of this elevation of self above the level of others.

But in fact no one, not even God (in the incarnation, especially not God), claims to be above humanity to the extent that the prideful person often does.

Perhaps the proudest person I have ever been close to on a regular basis is a young woman whom I saw for several years. In her first five minutes inside our door she alienated the secretary by refusing to fill out the forms everyone else fills out. She scoffed at a resident for suggesting she follow the same rules as other people, argued about the fee, and took over territory that usually belonged to the staff. After involving the therapist in the standard verbal fencing, she spun out a series of tales over several months in which her placing herself above the neighbor was everywhere obvious: in sexual conquests, rude insults, goading employers to the limit of their tolerance, and stretching the edges of the therapy contract with lateness, cancellations, drugs, and attempts to compromise the therapist. In her vocational life this woman not only considered herself the best physician there was, but was cruelly and openly derisive of others with whom she had to work, and would quickly move from institution to institution because the people and practices nowhere were good enough to command her respect. In personal relationships her demand for adoration was so high that when friends or lovers would spend a few minutes listening to someone else, they would find themselves the butt of a publicly embarrassing demand for attention and deference. No one else's feelings were as worthy of being considered as hers.

A fitting contrast for this paragon of pride is the humility of a modern Christian saint like Dom Helder Câmara of Brazil. Dom Helder is archbishop of Recife in northeastern Brazil, a region of great poverty and crowding in the narrow strip of coastal plain where the cities are hemmed in against the sea. He has been a leader in the struggle against exploitation of the poor, and as such has become a vocal and hated enemy of the government. He has refused to live in the plush diocesan residence, and has turned it into a community center for the people of his city. But these are not the things that are most remarkable about this man. His impressiveness springs largely from his refusal to be impressed with himself, his willingness to be seen as a buffoon, a clown who picks up little children and throws himself into the spirit of public events with a childlike and obvious delight. Despite his great power, high position, and international reputation, he allows his joy to show in his giving over of himself to the situation around him, be it by tapping his feet and waving his arms in time with the music in a parade or embracing César Chavez at a mass in the lettuce fields of southern California. Here is a man who places himself above no one, and yet despite himself is often held to be first of all.

But this exemplar of Christian humility does not achieve that status by self-conscious attempts to restrain his pride, which is a typical Christian strategy. I had a fascinating experience that made me keenly aware of that method. I was with a group of clergy in a southern Indiana city, using an exercise designed to help persons make a realistic assessment of their impact on others. When I asked these clergy to line up in the order of the influence they had in this group, with the most influential at the north end of the room and the least at the south, they all jostled and pushed to see who could get closest to the south wall. Yet one of the members of that group was looked up to by his colleagues as a writer and lecturer, another was pastor of the largest church in the community, another was chairperson of the ministerial association, etc. The poor man who was left standing closest to the north end of the room, and therefore presumably the most influential, was in fact the person who could least convince his colleagues that he should be allowed closer to the holier low end of the totem pole. When we processed this exercise, the group showed they were offended that they would be asked to violate what they understood to be the Christian mandate to place no person lower than themselves. When I asked them to line up without reference to that concern, the rankings were almost the reverse of what they had been before. The pride in this group showed in the competition to be seen as least prideful.

True humility is not the studied attempt to avoid believing, or to avoid letting anyone else know you believe, that you have power, influence, excellence, reputation, or anything else. It is, rather, to be where you are as though your status were not as important as what you do with it in the treatment of other persons. To pour out energy in the attempt to be seen as the most humble is as prideful as to pour it out in the attempt to be seen as king. It has been written that true humility is to remember that one is a prince or a princess, the child of a king, and that the greatest of sins is to forget it. Or, as Karl Olsson puts it, "Humbleness is seen to be not sham modesty but a creative excitement about the presence of God."[5] How do we lose this excitement, this humility, and puff up our spirits in the sin of pride? What is it that we seek that gets us into such dangerous territory?

Pride begins in our uncertainty as a child that we will be granted a place, that anyone will endorse and defend our right to the few cubic feet of the cosmos that we occupy. Our belief that we are, or ought to be, larger than life develops naturally in a situation where great size or importance would provide the only safety. The prideful adult's childhood is often like that of the woman physician I men-

tioned earlier. Feeling a constant struggle for the right to
be—in the face of a mother who had to have the total attention of everyone around her or else try to drive them off—
our young woman as a child first attempted to provide that
attention. When she found out that no amount of attention
was enough, she grew hardened to her mother's recurrent
condemnations and tried to find love from an often absent
father instead. But during his absences her mother's extrav-
agant demands, and the vicious punitiveness that surfaced
when those were not met, left my client with no certainty at
all that her place would still be there for her at the end of
the day. When one is in that position, one learns quickly to
view any human contact as potentially dangerous unless
one's power is unopposed.

To be a child in this position is to live in chronic fear that
your hold on your place in family and world will be lost; and
you are also constantly on the lookout for a way to guarantee it. It is this search that is responsible for the elation you
feel upon first learning a skill you can perform markedly
above the level of other children. Here is your guarantee of
a place, the thing you can do or be so well that the others
can't get along without you. If you can only maintain that
excellence, they will never be able to get rid of you, and
your security is assured.

Any competence or quality can play this crucial role. A
fetching smile and flashing eyes, early ability to read or tell
time, the capacity to pound a nail straight or throw a ball,
all can suffice. Some skills, of course, quickly become com-
monplace as other children learn them, though qualities
like physical beauty take much longer to lose their power.
One needs to capitalize on one's abilities by pushing them
into greater and greater achievements, since ordinary skills
will have no currency at all after a few months or years. The
child whose early strokes come from having the best hand-
writing in the second grade may be out of luck three years
later. But most of us learn that, having established our claim

to pride with our beauty, coordination, strength, artistic imagination, or ability to think and remember, we can continually push those attributes into new areas of accomplishment as we become older and live in more complicated worlds.

Imagine that this once-reliable ability is called into question by a critic or a competitor. Someone says we aren't doing it right, or someone else appears who does it better. What happens to our confidence that our place in the world is secure? This challenge strongly tempts most of us to try to preserve self-confidence by declaring ourselves to be above the discussion, and either refusing to consider the criticism or denying that the competitor should be taken seriously. In childhood and youth, we often can't pull that off successfully. The critic often has a lot more power than we have (typically being a parent or a teacher), and the competitor may demonstrate the weakness of our claim by besting us at the contest. Childhood pride is an on-again, off-again proposition for most, since children are regularly thrust into more and more demanding competition and being reviewed by critics with higher and higher standards. It is only the few who always win and always satisfy the critics.

Those few, if they are skilled at an accomplishment that continues to be useful throughout life, join a small number of others to become the most dedicated victims of mature pride. The others are those who largely failed in childhood, or repeatedly had to change their game when their competence was too limited, but who finally found an area of adult achievement in which their skill guarantees them a place. These prideful ones are those whose accomplishments can pass muster, whose competitors and critics must grant that they have a right to their place; which therefore makes them vulnerable to the danger of being overly impressed with the accomplishment. The more frustrating the early failures, the more intense the adult pride. It is said that pride is ultimately the sin of the virtuous and the successful, and so it is, for those with more obvious failings are constantly having their pride shattered. It is those who have excelled, who have done well enough that they have not had to give up the hope for realistic pride, who are in the greatest danger from it.

For that reason I have to argue with the traditional judgment that pride is chronologically the first of sins. For most of us as young children (once we have it clear that we are separate from our mothers) our sense of power and competence is very limited, and we spend a substantial amount of our time being unsure we can count on our rights to anything. Much of our early sin comes from our exaggerated sense of weakness and our resulting scramble for the goods we need to survive, not from an exaggerated sense of our rights that leads us to defy God or the neighbor. The traditional position—pride as the first of sins—makes more sense for an adult, since almost all of us as adults have some areas in which we feel a proprietary right. And for this sin to be effective, that area need not be large or public. It can be as minimal as the claim to have the undisputed right to make decisions about matters of purely private concern, which in turn produces our angry rejection of any claim that we need to consider other viewpoints or interests. In that stance, having reserved unto ourselves the right to decide unilaterally, we more easily fall into avarice, vengefulness, envy, etc. But those sins have independent sources, and though they may be fed by whatever immature pride we develop early in life, they have their own strength and do not depend on pridefulness for a beginning.

But let us return to the prideful, competent, successful adult. Suppose I have developed my competence and nursed my pride to assure myself a place in the world. But I have a critic: someone who believes that I should be performing my prided function in some other way. (It should be noted that no one of us is exempt from that message, since no human effort can be assumed to be perfect.) Since I have built my security on the fulfillment of the function, to hear that message is to be in danger of having to change my entire way of life. It is so much easier to decide that the critic fails to understand a crucial point, that her or his credentials are insufficient, or that no one at that level of skill should be allowed to criticize a person at my level. The same is true of the competitor, who at this level is always an implied critic. The competitor's criticism, the unspoken complaint in his or her very willingness to do things in a different way, can be readily dismissed if I conclude I am in fact superior and need not pay attention.

It is this dismissing that is the greatest loss the sin of pride causes the prideful person. It takes me out of fellowship and weakens the very contribution that sustains my self-respect. If I do not hear my critics—which I must not, if to hear them is to doubt my place in the world—then I cannot use their criticism to improve my work. That's an especially touchy problem for the prideful person of a respected profession or position, for to such a person criticism almost always comes from below (where almost everyone else is)—from one's clients, one's competitors, one's children, even one's less informed and successful neighbors and fellow church members. Since to hear would be to abandon the secure place that is above the others, pride often chooses not to hear and thereby loses the ability to maintain its excellence. That is especially fatal in ministry and psychotherapy, where it is only by hearing—even the unpleasant—that excellence exists.

So not only is excellence lost, but also fellowship. If I cannot hear your real or potential word to me about the most important areas of my life, I shut you off from the chance to touch me where it would do me the most good. Hence, the core of me, that which I most count on to secure my place in the world, remains frightened and alone, unable ultimately to either give or get in the life-sustaining dia-

logue with the neighbor. It is from this failure of fellowship
that the most grievous abuses of human beings develop. We
see this in the mother who maims her child in retaliation
against the child's daring to share its anger; we see it in the
police officer who lashes out brutally against the citizen who
challenges her right to make arbitrary decisions; and we see
it in the religious leader who vilifies as unchristian and
immoral those who differ with his own position.

But unfortunately the individual level is not the only
locus of prideful destruction. The refusal to hear the other,
and the resulting ignorance about what the other truly is,
is practiced at the social, cultural, and political levels with
chilling and devastating results. Even those of us who individually are too inept or too humble to venture into pride
find ourselves exultantly throwing our weight behind corporate, religious, racial, or national pride in a way that
makes us part of a lethal juggernaut. History is filled with
the casualties of prideful ignorance; untold thousands of
southern blacks and their supporters early in this century in
the United States; the Vietnamese people later in the century; the Jews of Europe in the 1930s and '40s; Native
Americans throughout the previous century and beyond;
the Armenians, the Cambodians, the Aztecs, and practically
every other group that has been identifiable and not powerful enough to defend itself.

We seem to be particularly vulnerable to this way of destruction at the places and in the communities we consider
most holy. Hence, the Christians refused to hear and, therefore, to know or love the Jews; the capitalists refuse to hear
the communists, who in turn refuse to hear the capitalists;
the Democrats refuse to hear the criticisms of the Republi-
cans, who are similarly deaf to the Democrats; and the psy-
chiatrists refuse to hear the psychologists who refuse to
hear the social workers who refuse to hear the pastoral
counselors, and Blue Cross refuses to hear them all.

It seems that our most trusted institutions, when they

have given us places in the world we could not win as individuals, give us the most powerful opportunity to rupture the human fabric. Who has not felt brutalized at the hand of some government clerk who believes his or her secure job carries with it the right to refuse to hear either the most reasoned or the most impassioned complaint? Who has not seen some religious fool (defined as someone whose position disagrees with yours) piously demand that another human being's rights be taken away? Who has not been folded, spindled, or mutilated at the self-satisfied hands of some ribbon clerk carrying out the will of a corporate computer?

Pride promotes the destructive clinging to last year's way of doing it, which is the way we have already perfected. It is only the ability to put pride aside that allows us to hear this year's challenge and develop next year's solution. So pride mires us in an ignorance that builds great institutions around itself, considering it a crime to see any new truth. It keeps us, so far as it has power, a step and sometimes farther behind the awareness that could help us deal with the actuality of our world. It keeps us forever subject to the power of those so addicted to power that they prefer it to truth. And it makes our own motives highly suspect when we would attempt to overthrow them, for it is all but impossible to know when it is passion for truth that impels us and when it is pride of place.

In fact, every shred of new awareness of our world must fight its way in against the prideful resistance of some human being, and then, through that person's efforts, against the prideful resistance of the organized forces that are invested in seeing things the way they have always been seen. The best of us are in that trap, and can never completely leave it without abandoning the faith in a structured universe that keeps us sane. But that sanity is bought at a price, the price of the systematic and painful suppression of the new and of those who would be its bearers.

Each of us has despaired from time to time of having a place that matters in the world. Each of us has struggled to develop some skill or knowledge or essence that entitles us to a claim for it. Each of us requires some measure of that certainty to relax and make whatever contribution we make to the world. None is immune to the need. Hence, none avoids pride, the sinful overgrowth of that necessity to a point where we believe that it and we are above reproach. Avoiding it is not an option. Only allowing it to be redeemed can save us.

How do we seek to diminish the role of pride in our lives and in the lives of those for whom we have responsibility? To begin with, there is the preventive function we can play in the lives of those who depend on us, our children, pupils, clients, and friends. What we can do for them is simply to grant them a place and be sure they know that it is a gift to them. When there is certainty that I can be here and you will want me, there is no need to earn it; therefore no need to defiantly defend the claim that it has been earned. There are therefore no conditions that I must meet to deserve it, and that I can claim to have met so that you owe it to me. It is not owed to me or to anyone else; it is a gift. It is my gift to my children, yours to your students or clients, God's to all of us.

This has serious implications for the ways we handle situations in which our children and others fail to do as well as we would like. Whatever the message to them is, it must include the statement, explicit or implicit, that neither this failing nor any other compromises your standing in this family, in this therapy, in this class. It means that anger, when it comes, must be demonstrably a product of your commitment to the other, rather than a threat to withdraw your commitment. It means that unavoidable displacements, such as marital separation or other family crisis, must be handled so that the children are assured that they have a place with all the people they formerly belonged with. Only then can they count on the certainty that they are grounded in their universe in a place that is given to them; only then can they be spared the temptation of having to believe that they earned that place and have a right to defend it against all competition or criticism.

But when we are the prideful ones, and it is in ourselves that we suspect this cancer to be growing, the prescriptions do not come as easily. There are, however, several steps I can suggest if you suspect it is a primary dilemma of your own. The first would be to listen very closely to your critics. This is especially necessary when the message is disagreeable, or when there is some strategic advantage to be lost if you hear it and believe it. For most people this is especially difficult when the stakes are high—as, for instance, in the chronic, repeated arguments on the same subject that rest somewhere in even the best of marriages. (How I hate to hear my wife say that I don't require enough responsibility from our children! Part of why I hate to hear it is because I suspect she is right.) The same vigilance is especially necessary in work situations, where the message from any one particular colleague is likely to be the same month in and month out, and is also likely to bear the stamp of truth that comes from long familiarity. This also is a factor in situations of review and judgment: job evaluations, site visit reviews, membership hearings, legal proceedings, etc. Anywhere that the stakes are high, and where what is said may force a reassessment of an area in which we thought we were above criticism, needs to have special attention if we seek redemption from our pride. Not that we should always agree, but it is very important to our well-being that we listen, that the message of the other gets all the way inside us where it can be assessed on the basis of the evidence.

As a special step toward pulling off this tricky task, we do well to identify those general classes of situations in which we are likely to be defensive and fail to hear. I listed some of them above, but I suspect that they are different for different ones of us. I may be accurately confident that the message in my job evaluation is going to be positive, but I may need to listen with special care if a site reviewing team comes to examine my training program.

Vulnerable points are different for different ones of us, but we all have them. One particularly useful strategy in those situations is to enlist more than one set of ears. If I think I am going to have trouble hearing what a visiting team may say to me, I had better take along a colleague whose hearing I trust. Perhaps a tape recording of the stress interview situation will give me a better opportunity to hear it later when my anxiety is lower, or when a trusted colleague can listen with me. Another useful tactic is to warn the expected speaker that I may have trouble hearing, so she or he can be alert to indications that the message is not getting through, and check that out with me from time to time. I may want to carry the results of the encounter, and the data on which they are based, to review with my pastor, my therapist, my supervisor, or someone else whose objectivity and goodwill I trust. I would do well in such situations not to expect this protection from my pride from a person I think I may have in my pocket. This is not a good time to ask for clarification from an employee, a spouse who never challenges, or anyone else whose advantage is served by flattering us. Flattery will not help our struggle with pride.

Once you have done what you can to alert yourself to your own selective deafness, and to immunize yourself in the most dangerous situations, there is a set of questions you should ask yourself about any message you suspect pride is making difficult to hear. The first question is this: "If the speaker is right, and I fail to hear, what will it cost me?" The second is like the first: "If I really do let this message in, what effect is it going to have?"

Let's give some attention to the first of these. If pride would keep you from hearing a message, usually the long-range cost of refusing to hear it will be great. If I fail to hear my wife in a regular objection, inevitably her faith in my willingness to share an ongoing dialogue will diminish. As that sinks, so does my certainty that I can count on her to tell me the things that need to be said. If I fail to hear a critical message in a job evaluation, or refuse to believe that it's true, my employer is left with only more drastic measures for expressing displeasure. I may find myself out on my ear. If a site reviewing committee tells me that certain things are amiss in the work of my training program, and I fail to hear or respond, the quality of my work is going to suffer, and with it its reputation and ability to attract students. Furthermore, the respect I hope to have from those who do the reviewing will inevitably be diminished. There are comparable costs for every such message that pride prevents my hearing.

But the more difficult question to cope with is the cost of hearing well. If I have built my reputation on an ability to see deeply into the subtleties of the character of deeply disturbed persons, and someone says flatly that I'm just too easy on these people and they need to be dealt with more firmly, a crucial underpinning of my approach to my work and my view of myself has been jarred. If I examine the cost of hearing such a message, and if I find that it would be great, then what I must do to escape bondage to my pride becomes clearer. I would have to examine closely the quality of my work with persons I thought I had helped the most. I would have to question whether my reputation was built on work of good quality, or whether I had misled dozens or hundreds of people who believed what I said about such situations. When the stakes are that high, it's all but impossible for my pride not to be involved. Then I simply must get some other opinions.

This question presses immediately beyond itself to a subsequent set of issues. If, in fact, the cost of hearing any particular message is very great, if it strikes at the root of what we consider to be of value about ourselves, then the dangers of pride are great. We can control them somewhat in the way a city seeks to immunize itself against financial depression: we can broaden the base. If your main claim to a place in the world is the work you do with seriously disturbed clients, you might also become an expert supervisor of beginning therapists. If one is taken from you or shattered by criticism, the other remains. This is a method of preserving ourselves against the temptation to place all our eggs in one basket and then to fight to the death for that basket. To some extent this method is available to everyone, for who is there without more than one skill worth mentioning? But each of these individual skills is vulnerable to the same questioning, and we are likely to find that any truly cogent critique of our functioning in one of these areas shows up in similar ways in every other. Even if we are established in the world in a number of ways, our vulnerability is diminished only quantitatively, not qualitatively.

Ultimately, when the cost of hearing the word pushes us to the utmost, we are thrown back on our ability to endure the fear that we could lose our rightful claim to an honored place in the world. To strengthen ourselves we must look at the grief and fear we would feel if we were successfully challenged on the most precious of our repertoire of skills. That would return us to the original situation we faced as children, not being sure how we are placed in the world. The loss of our confidently held claims would certainly leave us shaky, frightened, and sad. Until we have explored, at least in our imaginations, whether we could survive such a loss, it is unlikely that we would be able to stand against our own pride and keep our ears open in the face of messages, actual or potential, that we would hate to hear. The only way to be sure we could allow ourselves such pain is if we have developed an ability to trust greater than what we had when we first learned to be proud. Without the confidence that somehow the world, those who love us, or God would sustain us in the absence of the abilities and position we thought made us invulnerable, we could hardly afford to open ourselves to the neighbor.

We are ultimately on this earth in the same predicament that our children are in our families. We have a place only because it is given to us, whether that gift comes from God, from our parents, or from some impersonal force. None of us have earned it, and our ability to earn it now has no effect on its having been made available in the first place. Perhaps those who see their place as the gift of a loving God are in a better position to trust that their vulnerability would not be taken advantage of if they were successfully criticized, but that instead they could find some new basis on which to establish their stance in fellowship with those around them. If our place has been given us by an unassailable power, everything that we have earned, all that we could rightfully be proud of, could be taken. We would still have our place, because that is not of our own making.

The anxious clutching to a superiority we have achieved by our own strength is only necessary when we do not trust the dependability of the place we have been given. And perhaps to ask for that trust is to ask for the hardest test of all, the concession that all we have achieved does not make us different from, or more secure than, the lowliest of God's creatures. What we have a right to claim as our permanent possession is only that which has been given, which is ultimately far grander than anything we can achieve by our merit. How humbling it is—perhaps impossibly humbling—to think that all the wisdom that has been educated into us, all the success that we have managed, all the benevolence that we have performed, is ultimately as nothing next to that which we share with the lowliest beggar: our humanity and its redeemability at the hands of a loving God. When that can be embraced, our inevitable slippage into pride can always be restored. It can be something we laugh at and with, as we would laugh at and with a child who stumbles gently into a pile of cushions while learning to walk. It can be part of the human frailty that makes us lovable. Without the willingness to allow ourselves to be redeemed, to allow ourselves to be humbled by knowing the insufficiency of our finest efforts, that same flaw can grow into the murderous monster that perpetuates the Holocausts of history.

We should know that from time to time we will refuse to hear. We should prepare ourselves by identifying the situations in which our not hearing is most likely. We should ask the cost of not hearing and face the price of hearing well. And we should trust that, even if we do hear and are shorn of our pride, we rest ultimately in the good graces of a power that freely grants us far more than we can ever achieve by our striving.

# PART V

# Sin and the Christian Life

---

# 9. The Physiology
# and Sociology of Sin

One of the conclusions of this book, as well as of the Christian gospel, is that sin is a part of every life. "All have sinned," Paul writes, and I am ready to concede that all will sin. The utter exclusion of sin is not a human possibility, and the attempt to live defensively in the hope of preventing it produces more sin rather than less. Even worse than that, it saps energy and creativity in such a way that the amount of good a person accomplishes is shrunken.

The best strategy for dealing with sin in Christian life is not to make a resolute attempt to exclude it, but to seek the goals of the abundant life well and powerfully enough that sin is not necessary to make life interesting and to give it the appearance of being enjoyable. We won't completely root sin out by that method, but we will structure our existence so that most of our energy flows into achievement of the good ends that God has put here for us. Sin will get the leftovers, the occasional missteps rather than having our entire store of energy invested in it through the attempt to avoid.

Remember the parable of the talents! The one-talent man, who hid his treasure in the ground to avoid making a mistake with it, is the one whom Jesus rebukes. The one who invested all of it and ran the risk of a grievous loss, but whose fear of the loss did not paralyze his action, was rewarded. And so it is in life. Those who will to live it, who seek its rewards wholeheartedly, knowing that they may err and suffer or even deal out pain, are those who give the most to their neighbors and have the fullest lives for themselves. Those whose existence is dominated by avoidance tend to shrivel and neither give nor achieve much.

An old country and western song captures the wisdom of life that Martin Luther first made famous in his advice to "sin boldly." It testifies: "I'd rather be sorry for something I've done, than for something I didn't do."

## A Longitudinal View of Sin

Sin always begins in the natural desire for some good thing. Much of its power and its danger comes from the impossibility of telling the difference between a sinful desire and a noble one. It is not the hunger, the fatigue, the sexual longing, or the wish to exercise an influence that is wrong, but what is done on the basis of the desiring.

In fact, not only are the desires that lead us into sin natural, they are necessary; we must fulfill them if we are to live the lives God intended us to live. And we know it, we sense the danger to our selfhood if we don't eat or rest, defend ourselves, or acquire at least a few possessions. Feeling that necessity, we rightly increase our efforts and focus them in these seven areas, trying to get the right balance of comfort and challenge for life.

All of that is good. The problem begins when we sense ourselves failing in our quest to get enough rest, enough established individual selfhood, enough sexual satisfaction, etc. In that situation, when we fear that our natural and unstrained capacities won't be sufficient to bring in the prize, we become a little desperate. We so intensify our focus on the specific commodity in question that we lose sight of the people around us and their needs, of our own competing priorities, and of the balance in our own lives. We struggle, increasingly blindly, to get whatever the goal is that we have told ourselves will make us safe (or contented, or happy, or whatever), gradually losing touch with the effects of our efforts.

If we are successful in this uneasy attempt, we become vulnerable to a further complication. Having gained the prize at such cost and with so much uncertainty, we are unwilling to relax the vigilance with which we hold on to it; and having felt so satisfied at having won, we predictably expect to feel even more satisfied to repeat the victory. So we cling to the reward so hard and long that we fail to notice when it is time to start seeking a different one, often organizing our lives around the repetition of a struggle we have already proven to ourselves we can win. In the process, the newness of life gets away, as we remain preoccupied with demonstrating our habitual mastery, not noticing that there are new struggles ahead in which our victories are not so certain. And if we do notice them, we may continue to prefer the ones we know we will win.

So we hold on to our good thing too long, seek it too single-mindedly. That is the essence of our sin. "Time makes ancient good uncouth," says a familiar hymn, and theology has told us for generations that an act that was the will of God yesterday may be an obstacle in the divine path today.

Note that the fly in this particular ointment is not the desiring but the fear that the desiring will not be satisfied. The sin occurs at the intersection where the God-given and necessary wish pushes on us from one side, and the lack of skill, confidence, or faith that we know how to get the things we must have blocks us on the other. In that particular pinch it is understandable, if deadly, that we sometimes feel compelled to coerce or deceive the neighbor, misuse and blind ourselves, in order to reach the goal we feel we must reach.

The result of this sinful fixation on the battles we know we can win is a kind of idolatry that makes the achievement of this specific one of life's goods the only objective that matters. In this idolatry we see forty-year-old adolescents believing that a continual stream of new sexual partners is what makes life worth living, and that if they can get that, nothing can possibly hurt them. I suspect another example lurks a few feet in front of every bumper sticker that reads "I don't get mad, I just get even," the proclamation that the driver's identity is linked to the angry ability to intimidate everyone else and keep them away from what she or he has proclaimed as personal territory. And we are all familiar with those who have made gods of power or wealth and see no point in anything else.

There is a peculiarly powerful reverberation from this kind of idolatry. When we practice it, whether it concerns a fine wine or the power to move nations, we almost always dream up a story that makes us believe that whatever achievements lesser mortals manage, they count for little when compared to our own excellence. If we believe our own story, we then can believe that what we have done is the greatest thing we could do, and we need neither change nor find any new worlds to conquer. If we do that alone, then the only ones hurt are ourselves and those we have wounded en route to our goals. But we are rarely content to do it alone. We understandably organize ourselves and others who share the same idolatry to proclaim it as the summit of human achievement and ourselves as the mountaineers who have climbed it. Thus organized, we are a more formidable danger. Others who are still free of idolatry are often persuaded that it is unsafe not to follow us, if we are successful with our public relations and advertising. And we may gain enough outright power to change or strengthen the rules under which others must seek the goods they value. When our own idolatries are narrow, that poses a dangerous threat to human freedom and the quality of every community. The combination of pride of power and of racial purity, for instance, has spawned most of the genocides of history—and not even a little idolatry is safe.

That's ironic, for it is the search for a perfect, or at least a dependable, safety that often powers the idolatry. It is our wish for insurance—run rampant, so to speak—that most makes the real safety unavailable. Once we have achieved a given good, perhaps in the face of severe opposition, it is natural to want to keep it. It is even understandable that, in the effort to maintain it, we would lose sight of the other possible goods that can be enjoyed. But when we succumb to that wanting, and the energy that goes into holding on to the present safety is greater than that going into the expansion of life, we are in danger of losing not only those future goods but the present good we are trying to keep as well.

Not only does that concentration on safety cripple our reaching out into the world, it activates a dangerous response from the neighbor. Suppose your next-door neighbor, in whom you have had only a modest interest, suddenly begins building high walls between his property and your own, acting for all the world as though he must protect his safety from an attack he expects from you. Not only are you likely to suspect he has gone a little berserk, you are likely to find yourself becoming angry with and suspicious of him. Your chance for fruitful cooperation with him shrinks, and the likelihood that you will begin to expect evil from him grows; you may even become angry enough about his distrust to become a danger to him.

That's the way our preoccupation with the safety of the goods we have achieved affects other people. It creates enemies, while at the same time cramping our own capacity to live. Anytime we find ourselves focusing on the safety and repeatability of the life we have, we are vulnerable to this doubly damning effect of sin.

The compounding of evil does not stop there. Typically, when we get preoccupied with maintaining the safety of the goods we know how to get, we bring considerable pressure to bear on ourselves and those around us to get and keep them. More and more our life is marked by situations in which we are making ourselves, or someone else, do something that will increase that safety; less and less do we find ourselves or others doing good things for us out of the desire to do so. With all that forcing, so common in the neurotic patterns that pastoral counselors often treat, the spontaneity and freedom of life is forgotten. People even forget how to ask themselves whether they like what they're doing, whether they are happy. They often remember only to ask whether they are doing what they "must" do. "Must do—or else what?" I often ask. This kind of forcing has a particularly damaging effect on less-powerful people around us, especially our own children, who get the message that it's not what makes them happy that is important, but what they must do to avoid endangering the security and embarrassing the power of the adults around them.

Like the preoccupation with safety, the accompanying preoccupation with power summons a powerful response from the neighbor. People don't like or trust those who strive visibly to have more power than they do, any more than they like those who struggle to be safe from them. It invites them to try to match the power, which in turn becomes a lure to the neighbor's own sinfulness. Has anyone in an organizational structure escaped feeling that danger in the flesh? It is probably unsafe to allow the next guy or gal to actually get more power than you have, so the attempt to equalize the power is natural and even good. But if one of your co-workers interprets that as an attempt to endanger her, then her grasping for the resources to control will set off still another round. Witness the arms limitation talks, or the negotiations between any set of unions and managers.

In the process, the use of human and natural resources gets tragically skewed. When sin is dominant, the combination of tactics designed to preserve this or that privilege, safety, or power creates a tight set of boundaries, with all the energy going into keeping the potential enemy out of my territory and me from noticing what I'm doing. The natural flow of life is sapped and channeled into a network of squares like a checkerboard or a rice paddy. Little is left to pursue creativity or just routine goodness and fulfillment, since the available energy is exhausted before even the visible challenges and dangers can be removed.

That's why we have situations in nations where so much money and energy is spent trying (unsuccessfully) to stamp out prostitution that no funds are left to educate children sexually. There are marriages where the investment in determining who is running the show out-competes enjoying each other. And too many individual lives, cramped by being sure no one infringes on their authority, are without energy for love.

Our standard tactic of attempting to avoid sin by inhibiting ourselves fits perfectly into this picture. Our focus and investment in avoiding the sin sets up and/or reinforces the same boundaries as our preoccupation with safety and power, and it may be simply another way to be safe and powerful with others and ourselves. Life becomes centered on preventing certain things from happening, and the things can as easily be lust or anger as someone else's intrusion or our own laxity. It is even possible that the rigorous attempt to inhibit ourselves and avoid a specific sin—lust or gluttony, for instance—is a way of strengthening our bondage to another sin, such as pride or covetousness.

Let's look quickly at how that might work. Consider a woman who has invested the bulk of her life's energy in the acquisition of property. She is deeply entwined in covetousness, though being outwardly a highly moral person. That commitment to property naturally helps her identify possible dangers to her ability to keep what she has gained. One way to do that is to work hard, long, and carefully, while keeping at least one eye open to possible thieves and con artists. That way of structuring life leaves little room for love, no time and space in which it could happen. She might occasionally think an outraged thought at newspaper accounts of teen-age pregnancies or the sexual liberalization of the society, confident that her sexual purity is the greatest of excellence. She may spurn prospective suitors, especially if their interest is noticeably physical, telling herself that other people may need that sort of thing, but she, fortunately, is above it. She may even offer occasional advice to young people in her church about the dangers of dating too early or vigorously, and most probably she will be highly critical of employees who refuse to work late because they want to be home with their wives or husbands. Her amassing of wealth will increase, her covetousness deepen, and the intensity of her own lust that breaks through whenever her repression slips will grow more powerful. Her avoidance of sin (lust) by the inhibition of her own natural longings, forcing herself to a safety that does not admit them to consciousness, will plunge her deeper into a sin she has not identified (avarice) and increase her ultimate vulnerability to the sin she sees herself as safe against.

To summarize, sin always develops out of the desire for some good thing, which we have learned to get only desperately and uncertainly. We decide that we shall never give up that good, since life without it would not be worth having or capable of being maintained. So we make an idol of it, organize life around keeping it safe, force ourselves into channels that distract awareness from the process and force others into patterns of relating to us that protect our fearful vulnerability. We divert our energy from the ongoing dance of life to secure the ability to repeat these particular steps, and we seal off the whole process by forgetting we've done it and labeling the next possible steps of the dance as evil and dangerous—and a threat to the public good. And if we succeed, we wall ourselves up in slavery to our own sin, with one of the walls being the successful condemnation of others in their seeking to live out their lives, either in sin or in growth.

## THE ILLUSION OF AVOIDANCE

Much of our religious teaching has encouraged us to believe that if we are good enough, if we avoid doing the things we are supposed not to do, that we will be saved and life will be blessed. If the arguments of this book have made any impact on you, the reader, you know by now that these ancient beliefs are untrue. But how do they fail? What prevents our best intentions, our zealous struggles to be good, from making us happy or bringing about a humane world?

Some of that preventing has been clarified in the previous chapters and in the first part of this chapter; but there is a class of obstacles that lie beyond the conscious control of any individual. They are great societal patterns, institutions that survive because we as a culture have built particular sins into our everyday ways of doing and feeling, ways we inherit and are invited into at every new birth and each social contact. These obstacles require us to take measures that are beyond the scope of the previous chapters, and are as much the arena for political and ecclesiastical action as for moral choice.

### a. Our Crippling of Our Children

Each one of us emerged from childhood believing that some things are good and true which simply are not, the particular things differing for different ones of us. As long as those errors remain unexamined and active, they continue to lead us into sin and to be repeated in the way we raise our own children. Most of them are contained in particular maxims that were once useful, perhaps even true, but whose time has passed. Or they persist in habitual behaviors that once served the best possibilities reachable in a given situation, but have not changed with the situation.

They represented the best that was known at a given point
in our family's ancestral life, and are passed on to us as such,
but now are often obstacles to our ability to grow and respond to new situations.

Each of the seven sins has its own set of these obsolete
learnings, many of them given a semisacred standing by the
popular religion of this or some other time. Sloth, for instance, was meant to be prevented by the saying, "Idle
hands are the devil's tools," and in a frontier culture who
could argue? Even if you didn't like the theology, everybody
needed all possible productivity to survive, to reinvest, to
achieve a comfortable margin of safety. The saying itself
and the stoical indifference to the fatigue and pain it coun-
seled were a needed response to scarcity, and in the future
may become so again. But in the United States today a
bigger barrier to human fulfillment is the joyless preoccupation with producing more, working harder, filling more
time, often not because it is needed, but because following
the old maxim and leaving no time is a known way to
achieve psychological comfort. Ironically, then, the maxim
that once was intended to prevent a potentially dangerous
inactivity becomes precisely the stimulus to which a modern
child may respond slothfully, by learning merely to follow
orders and work dependently, since that is more comfortable and safer than responding to one's own needs or making
one's own decisions. That message, drummed over and
over again into one's mind as a child, can leave a person in
the lifelong situation of mistaking for sloth the needed and
creative remedies of rest and recreation, and of mistaking
actual dull-spirited sloth for industry and dedication.

For us as grown children to belatedly discover our own
and our parents' errors is both difficult and insufficient:
difficult because that which we have been taught to follow
religiously is contributing to our individual sin, and insufficient because it continues to be taught to other children,
perhaps even our own.

Our most important response to the discovery of such sin in us is a change in our child-rearing habits and in the popular morality we assist in passing on through the church. We cannot be held at fault for what our parents could not anticipate, and the time we have spent in any particular sin is a cause for sadness and repentance, not self-punishment. But we can change the way we affect the world as it grows up in the generations after us by passing on only those parts of our tradition which contribute to the blessedness of life in the situations our children and our churchfellows' children are most likely to face.

No one can possibly avoid being in sin for much of the time. We inherit huge amounts of it, or of the beliefs that make it inevitable when we live them out. Life changes faster than we do, and we may just painstakingly get something learned when a new revolution places it directly at cross-purposes with the movement of God in the world. Perfection, perfect innocence, is an illusion. Yet we must seek to follow the teachings of the past (they are the best we have), though we know that some of them will turn out to be wrong and to demand changing lest they cripple us utterly.

Throughout the book I have pointed out examples of child-raising practices that contribute to and perpetuate the sins. I'll pull these together here and add a few more that continue to undercut our efforts to humanize the world.

The real cripplers for sloth are the parental demands that interfere with the growth of initiative in the child, those add-ons following "Do what you're told" that suggest "— and nothing else." Especially crucial are parental insistence on doing all the thinking and deciding, punitive rebukes to real questions about reasons for decisions, subtle attempts to make the child so dependent on the parental approval and initiative that the ability to esteem the self is damaged.

Gluttony in its various forms is created by a childhood that gives the child no dependable supply of nurturing and care. When we refuse touch to a child, we encourage the child to find something to put in its mouth instead. When we won't look at or hear a child, a substitute comfort will be sought. But perhaps the most critical demands are those that make it dangerous for the child to attend to and value its own feelings, or even to believe they are real. "No, you're not tired (hungry, lonely, sad, etc.), you're . . ." The message that my feelings, the adult feelings, are the only ones that are important here makes it very difficult for the child to ever trust the messages from its own body that say that enough of something, be it food or drink or sex or whatever, is enough. Child-raising that anesthetizes the child's attention to its body, especially to its sense of pain and its wish to be cared for, breeds gluttony.

We will have vengeful children if their every mistake produces an outburst of blame that seeks more to hurt than to correct and restrain. Most child abusers were themselves abused as children, as were most prison inmates. Children who grow up believing that there is no way to count on justice in their most important relationships will be chronically angry, and will find a way to inflict their anger on someone who cannot even the score—just as they cannot. "Because I'm the boss" may be the biggest verbal invitation to long-standing anger, when flung by a parent whose right to decide has been unintentionally questioned by a child who wants to know how decisions are reached. Conversely, an excellent antidote to lasting anger is the dispassionate and consistent communication to the child that there is a cogent reason why we're doing things the way we are. Surprisingly, the refusal to allow childish anger does not uncomplicatedly produce adult vengefulness (though responding to it with explosive and punitive, provocative anger does). Instead, the refusal to allow it leads to sloth and depression, where the anger rots inside, killing initiative and hope.

Lust is best grown in families that are chaotic with lust,

on the one hand, or those in which moving toward another for touch and love is impossible, on the other. The chaos often comes from the union of lust and another sin, especially gluttony, anger, or envy, though all are candidates. In families where this combination is constantly moving partners out of one relationship and into another, allowing no building of deep human contact, children see and feel the lack of connectedness between the shifting partners and between parents and themselves. They long for the connectedness, and have had models that said sex is how you find it; but in their sex too, that which satisfies does not emerge. The same outcome is probable in families where child-rearing has emphasized shielding the children from all possible signs of potentially sexual contact, where all affection is outlawed because "the children are watching." A special contributor is our discomfort or outright anger at our children's masturbation, which for almost everyone is a necessary prerequisite to knowing the body well enough to involve it satisfyingly with another. We contribute most to the shrinking of lust when we make exploitative sex less interesting by modeling how rich and fulfilling committed sex can be; when sexual love is celebrated and enjoyed in ways that are reflected in every touch in a household and in every word about sexual matters. Then lust is outcompeted by a hearty sexual appetite paired with full respect for the partner.

The child-rearing that feeds covetousness happens in families that are more interested in things than in children. Ownership is a central concern in these homes, and things are more possessed than used. "That's mine" are the key words. It would be a mistake to look only to the wealthy for this evil, since a crust of bread can often be fought over as powerfully as a corporation. The antidote for covetousness is in the hearty enjoyment of objects, and the ability to shift when one object is gone to enjoy the next; in a context that always makes it clear that things serve people.

We teach our children envy when different family positions have grossly different privileges, either in freedom from duty or inclusion in love. If being the oldest, the youngest, the malest, the darkest, the prettiest, the richest, or whatever means that someone in your family gets treated differently than someone else, that "someone else" is going to learn to be envious at an early age. The saying "Boys will be boys," if quoted in the household, is often an early sign that girls in the same family will be envious. "Children should be seen and not heard" pointed to incipient envy for many children of an earlier generation. A rule requiring common respect for all persons, though that respect may be shown in different ways depending on different capacities, is the best guarantee that envy will not be built into the next generation.

The sin of pride is guaranteed by families who give no honor to any member, who regard self-love as so dangerous that even realistic praise is seen as evil. "Praise makes people lazy" could be heard in these homes, so that every member has doubts about being good enough to deserve his or her place. Conversely, "We're better than they are" is a message that makes prideful sin almost necessary to be in good standing. If you fear you're not good enough, then you'd better be better than somebody so in an emergency you can point that person out and deflect attention from your failure. The message that counteracts pride is, "You're just fine the way you are, but not better than anybody." If the first half is communicated powerfully enough, the last half is hardly necessary.

Most of us raise children the way we were raised. We have inherited our knowledge of how to do it, along with our own tendencies to sin and a deep loyalty to those who taught us. Often teachings that were necessary to survival in our parents' day are demonic in the present, but not because we mean to be evil when we do them. Our responsibility is to find the places in our lives where that is true and do what we can about it. But it takes more than a lifetime to find them all.

### b. Sins of Omission and Ignorance

We cannot know the consequences of all our deeds. It is beyond our ability to know which of the things we teach our children will be fruitful for them, and which of those that seem perfect for us will be destructive in their lives, just as the political and economic consequences around the world from our simplest acts may be far more intense than we realize.

This book has been about sins that the church saw as freely chosen acts, though I have tried to show that many of them are far from free. But for the most part, free or not, they are things we do. As such, they leave out a broad class of sins, the things "left undone that we ought to have done." Often our failure to act does more damage than our acting, if we are in a position to prevent an abuse of persons or environment and let it go unchallenged.

A particularly powerful form of omission, often used as the excuse for all the rest, is ignorance: "I didn't know the gun was loaded." Ignorance is tricky, because obviously none of us can know everything, and some of the things we need to know are known by no one at all. But we often hold on to ignorance, stubbornly using it as a shield against responsibility, to the point where we cannot find out what we need to know.

This is a special power of sin in large institutional structures, many of which survive only because no one knows their actual effects on human life. We learned as a nation in the 1960's that we are part of institutional racism, a powerful and deeply sinful situation, anytime we fail to find out the consequences of an act that affects blacks or other minorities. Buying a home, choosing a school, seeking a promotion, accepting a loan, all have unimagined effects. Not knowing the effects, we found life easier and less conflictual, but people were damaged. Knowing the effects would mean having enough information to go against the flow, to decide not to cooperate with the evil, which otherwise proceeds on unimpeded. Our ignorance is not random. The slothful man especially avoids finding out the consequences of his sloth, the envious woman avoids knowing what her envy produces. They will each be much clearer about the outcome of their occasional and rather minor vengefulness, and especially of the vengefulness of others. Ignorance protects the ability of the sinner to continue expecting to enjoy the sin. How much do we have to know? When can we justly stop trying to find out how our actions hurt other people?

There is probably no answer at all to that question, and if one could be developed, it would require another book. The point is that whenever we stop trying to know more about the consequences of our acts, we are in sin; and we all stop trying. None of us knows what we need to know, and none of us invests his or her entire life in trying to find out. Like the sins discussed in the rest of the book, our most fervent efforts to avoid ignorance will not fully succeed. Avoiding the evil simply won't do it. Even more importantly, we have to strive for the fullness of life.

All of us need to explore our lives for areas of unnecessary ignorance, especially when they are connected with centers of human pain. Ask yourself: Which of the groups of people who suffer in the world do I least know my effects upon? Is my ignorance necessary? Does that knowledge exist somewhere? Is there a reason, other than my sinfulness, for me not to know it?

### c. Corporate Sin—The Organization of Ignorance

Ignorance, of course, enables and supports the omission of action. If what is happening or not happening hurts you, but I don't know how, I can't be held accountable for not changing the situation. My sloth will keep me in my accustomed patterns. My omissions serve the same sins as my actions. I can vengefully kill my neighbor. With just as much vengefulness, I can stand aside and allow a stranger to do it.

But if I am artful enough in my vengeance, I can arrange to be far enough from the slaying and have enough intermediaries between that I can escape knowing it is happening. If I have some grudging admiration for the neighbor and some personal dislike for the trigger man, I can accomplish a dual objective: being rid of my inconvenient neighbor and feeling righteously outraged at the scum that did him in.

This is the beauty and the horror of our highly organized modern world. I don't have to know how to grow pineapples to be able to eat pineapples. And by an accomplishment as deft on the societal level as the creation of a neurosis in an individual, I don't even have to see what it does to the Hawaiian to have his land used for pineapples that I can eat. Someone else knows how to grow them. Someone else sees the pain of the harvester. They don't talk to me, and there is a sinful part of me that likes it that way.

The effects of these corporate sins is beautifully difficult to determine. With individual, active, conscious sin, it's fairly simple. When I am vengeful, covetous, proud, it is hard work to avoid noticing the effects it has on those around me; and very quickly I see that it also impoverishes me. My fulfillment shrinks when I seek it in individually sinful ways. But my involvement in collective sin is much more comforting. If I join a whites-only social club, take my children out of an integrated school, vote for lower taxes, buy mutual fund stock, fail to campaign actively in an election, etc., etc., I may rightly believe that those acts enhance at least my immediate individual satisfaction and that of my family and friends. But in each case it can also declare my membership in a group that is, at least potentially, poised over against another. As I enjoy my status and my income, my safety and my control of the future, I just as surely contribute to the impoverishment of the life of whole groups of others—others whom, conveniently, I for the most part never see.

I believe that we are utterly unable to be free of the responsibility and the effects of this type of sin. We are inescapably racist, sexist, ageist, nationalist, and subject to many other unnamed prejudices despite our noblest intentions. As members of the various groups we belong to we do damage to other people, and couldn't completely prevent it if we tried. This is true and would be true even if we never committed any of the aforementioned deadly seven. Ignorance and societal structures inescapably make it so.

But of course we do commit the other seven sins as well, and the combination is even more deadly. Our vengefulness or pride or covetousness may keep us from bothering to find out the effects of our corporate behavior, and these sins will certainly work against our doing anything with our new knowledge once we have it. But ignorance by itself can be partly dispelled, unless the other seven attack and kill the sources by which light can be brought to our situation.

There probably was a time when the management and stockholders of cigarette companies had no way of knowing the damage their product was doing. That was ignorance, and damaging enough. When they began to fight against the development of information that would let the question be judged, protecting their power, wealth, position, or whatever; and when they have fought up to the present time against informing people of the risks, that has compounded the damage done by ignorance and greatly increased the guilt.

Unfortunately we are always acting, as they did, with incomplete knowledge of the results of our action. When, as they did, we act with a certain success and develop large institutions and the power and wealth that go with them, our vulnerability balloons. When our initiative produces demonstrably dangerous results, by then thousands, even millions, of people have come to depend for the continuation of their way of life on that set of actions which is now demonstrated to be destructive. If we were only ignorant, we would repent and pay the price and try a different way to make a living. But more than ignorance is operative, so we struggle against knowing what we know, willing that others should die to preserve what we honestly built for ourselves. And since we never or rarely have to see the consequences close up, our inaction is understandable. But it is deeply evil and more destructive than all the individual lusting, coveting, and envying we can ever do.

The above example assumes no more than the average amount of individual evil in the beginning of the process. That is usually the case, since almost no one begins a course of action truly believing it is evil. But still the destructive power of those involved is immense, hideous, due largely to the inertia that any large group of people develops as it moves, and their ignorance of the consequences for those not involved. What is known clearly is the benefits of the action for those inside: in our example they are the farmers, the recipients of tax-supported services in tobacco-growing states, those who work in the distribution and manufacture of cigarettes, and those smokers for whom the dominant effects are still the calming and comfort of the smoke rather than the illness and limitations that come after years of consumption.

My purpose in introducing collective sin is not to treat it exhaustively. That would require another book. It is to reinforce the recurrent theme that even the most zealous attempts to avoid individual evil cannot eradicate sin and guilt, nor are they likely to make our world a great deal better to live in. And because of the crushing power of corporate evil, something does need to make our world better, or we could all be destroyed.

The weakness of the attempt to eradicate individual sin

by avoiding it, in addition to the fact that it doesn't work, is that it leads to the absorption of individual lives in patterns that don't challenge the powerful corporate evils that do endanger our world. The attempt to deal with individual sin by avoidance and inhibition is basically a conservative stance. It leads people to narrow the scope of life rather than to broaden it. But ignorance is too dangerous, especially ignorance of corporate evil. Anything narrowing the scope of life takes the person living it away from new knowledge and increases the domination of that ignorance. The result of that movement is the snowballing of the power of structures outside our awareness that damage the world.

Humanity desperately needs to broaden its knowledge, hence its control, over the forces that have such influence on how our lives are lived—be they governments, businesses, or informal, mutually reinforcing patterns of social habit. It is the nature of those structures to work against our understanding them, to convince us that they work more or less automatically and don't need our attention. And they often don't, if we like the consequences of their action. But if we dislike the consequences, if there are things that stem from them that we regard as corporate evil, we not only need to increase our knowledge and power in relation to them; we must do that against the resistance of our own inertia and their guile. It is not to the advantage of Liggett and Myers to have us know the effects of cigarette smoking. They won't help us find out.

In order to find out, and to learn the millions of other things we need to continue discovering in order to humanize life on this planet, we must adopt a stance toward evil that takes us into new territory and creates new awareness of its process and power. We must do that in a way that helps us transcend the pain that comes from the seven deadly individual sins and from the organized ignorance of corporate sin. That must be a stance that concentrates not primarily on the avoidance of evil but on the expansion of good—into the territory formerly dominated by evil. It is done only at the risk of being in situations where obvious temptation is much closer than the stance of avoidance allows, but where the opportunities for good, for joy, and for a truth that goes deep into the fabric of reality are more available than in any other way of living.

# 10. The Graceful Dance
## of Christian Life

Sin cripples and destroys life. Both the conscious, deliberate acts of the most cynical sinner practicing any of the deadly seven, and the ignorant omissions of which none of us is ever innocent—both can and do bring pain and prevent the growth of beauty.

This book has been a diagnostic manual for sin. If reading it has been instructive, you can now identify the ways you most often obstruct your God-given potential for wholeness. You can list your favorite sins, those that most often pretend to be the sources of happiness and most often trap you in their deceptions.

If you have diagnosed yourself, and if you want to diminish the hold your sin has on you, the change toward a graceful life has already begun. None of us ever achieves sinlessness, but when we accept what is in the world for us we can change our relationship to our sin. We can stop being slaves to it, with our sin dictating what we see and how we understand ourselves. We can begin being forgiven and forgiving, free and freeing persons. We may often be tripped up by our sin, but through a good not our own we can find the wisdom and strength to get up and continue in the direction that has been shown us. We struggle with sin, and sometimes are temporarily defeated by it, but it loses the power to define us in its terms. One stops being primarily a glutton, an envier, an avenger, and becomes primarily a forgiven Christian who periodically envies, is vengeful, or makes a pig of oneself.

Large parts of that process are beyond the scope of this writing. Suffice it to say that it is a gift of God, starting with creation and becoming particularly available to most of us in Jesus of Nazareth. That gift comes into individual lives in a simple and amazingly powerful way, marked by the recognition that the universe can be trusted; that there are things you can do in it that will work, and that if you do them, life will go reasonably well. It is true no matter how badly you have done before, if you make a clear-sighted attempt to know your own sin and change your life through the grace that is given us. Then the sin no longer owns you. The struggle with your imperfection will not end, but it is a struggle you can win with the help that is available. Life can be fulfilled, no matter what has already happened. But it can also be lost, so the turning (repentance) we're talking about has life-and-death importance. If it is undertaken, it can lead to a succession of changes that can make life both satisfying for you and a blessing to those around you.

How do you do it? Once the faith that love is supreme has taken root in you, the diagnosis of your major sin is the first step. Once that is done a major act of courage is required. You must remain faithful to the human longing, the wanting, that led you into that sin. In the attempt to avoid the sin you must not renounce the longing. That leads to avoidance and inhibition, the restriction (not the abundance) of life. You must stay with the longing until you know what it was you were seeking when you went off the track. Once you know, you must identify the major blocks to your getting it; it was in the faulty attempt to deal with those blocks that you chose tactics that got you into trouble. What do you know now that you did not know then about getting over that hurdle? What skill did you lack that led to your desperation? Can you learn it now? What despair did you succumb to, how were you convinced that you could never get what you felt you had to have? Could you learn to disbelieve the promises that you accepted in despair?

All of those questions have positive, hopeful answers. That's the basic message of the gospel. Some of the answers may require a lot of hard work to discover and even more to utilize. Psychotherapy, religious disciplines, careful educational efforts, may be required. But God has made no human being who cannot be redeemed. Anyone who exists can be fulfilled—by means that do not deepen her or his involvement in sin.

Once a person has come to know this, both life and the world are different. Read on and find the differences you can expect once you live beyond the sin that has bound you, if you can resist the temptation to renounce your longings.

## THE CREATION CAN BE TRUSTED

The basic theme of Christian life is trust, trust in the world in which we find ourselves, trust in its Creator, trust in ourselves. The creation is good, and our dominant attitude toward it need not be self-protection against its attacks or betrayals, but open and expectant exploration, playful curiosity fueled by the belief that most of the time there is some possible enjoyment and profit in what we find.

Erik Erikson, the psychoanalyst, pointed out that the hoped-for outcome of infancy for us all is basic trust, an attitude that leads us to expect that good things can come out of any encounter. On the basis of that attitude, young children continue to expand their world. They reach out, pull up, talk, play, and especially love. They also learn to trust themselves, if they are raised by trustworthy adults. They learn from adults' example that children too can be predictable, benevolent, and enjoyable. If children can, and adults can, it is reasonable to expect that the broader environment also can, within learnable limits. That confidence becomes the basis of the effort to learn what those limits are, what the structure of the world is. If you are pretty certain from your experience that things will make sense, it is easier to invest in finding out what sense they make.

Children without trust, raised by untrustworthy parents in an unpredictable situation, are more fearful, slower to believe in the possibility of useful knowledge, more content to limit what they know to a dependable safety.

Persons learn trust from trustable others. If God and the world cooperate for you and grace embraces you, a crucial consequence will be that you will see your feelings, longings, wishes, and emotions as part of that trustworthy creation. You will believe that when you want something, your wanting is a useful guide to what you actually need. You will believe that when you feel sad, it is because a real loss has occurred. You will believe that your anger usually means that you are in danger of being attacked or diminished.

This is immensely important. Because you trust the creation and your own naturalness as part of it, it means you know you have a usually reliable indicator of how things really are. If you feel anxious or angry or sad, it's a highly trustworthy sign that something needs to be done to change the situation you are in. If you feel O.K., it's time to slow down and smell the flowers. Our natural equipment carries in it better information sources than we are likely to find anywhere else. And it's a gift, free, available only for the cost of becoming aware of it and developing its power.

Admittedly, it is capable of being corrupted. We can sinfully block our sensitivity to ourselves and the world around us, most often when we fear we will be unable to get whatever it is we really want. Our blocked senses do become less reliable, but it is possible to know the difference between a message from our senses that is accurate and one that has been dulled or distorted by the fear that goes with sin. Sometimes there is no doubt that you are really hungry, and the certainty that goes with that can be developed for every other level of awareness.

Because the creation is trustworthy (and with it our own longings), our trust in God, the world, and ourselves gives us a way of regulating ourselves from the inside that is better than any possible method of getting it done from the outside. If we listen well, our bodies will tell us when we need to eat and drink and sleep and play and move around and laugh and cry and make love and run for our lives. We are born with that ability, but often we have learned not to feel the messages we give ourselves. We are taught that they are dangerous, that if we want the needed approval from parents and teachers, we had better pay more attention to what they want than to what we want, and we often completely lose the ability to notice when we want to do things. But we lose that ability at our great peril, for each of the seven deadly sins depends on our losing track of this natural self-regulation. If we notice when we are hungry and when we are full, we don't overeat; if we notice when we are craving someone's loving touch, we arrange to get it, and don't become lustful; if we notice our own anger promptly, we use it to rectify situations, and the need for vengefulness never develops.

One of the great tragedies of our faith is that many people use it to deny this very hope. They have been so frightened by the dangers of sin that, in their desperation, they have made rules more important than life. Jesus warned against this in his saying about the Sabbath being made for humanity and not vice versa, but sometimes when people or churches see the great evil any of these sins can produce, they understandably overreact in their determination to prevent it from damaging them again. And the rules that come from their reactions are often useful guidelines, each attempting to prevent an actual evil and preserve a real good, but the rules ultimately fail because they are clearer and simpler than life itself. The body, the seasons, the world, all change; the guidelines we develop must change also. When careful attention to the rule, whatever it is, replaces careful attention to life as it is in this body, no matter how obedient our behavior we inevitably will lose track of the ongoing life of God with persons. Self-fulfillment, which for a Christian must mean harmony with others, the world, and God, can only be achieved when one hears the tune that both they and oneself are singing.

Awareness, then, is another prime element of the life of grace. Fritz Perls wrote that awareness heals, by which he meant that it removes the ignorance about ourselves and our situations that keeps us feeling powerless and unsatisfied. Give human beings awareness of themselves in their environment, and you enable them to live powerfully for themselves and others. If the creation is trustworthy, to feel its reality and our own is both a pleasure and a means to create new things and events as they are needed to satisfy you and me.

If we are aware, and if we let the world be what it is, part of what we know and accept is finitude—the reality that our times, our skill, our knowledge, everything about us, is limited. Try as we might, we can only be who we are; not that and more. So much of sin is born of the attempt to get more than is possible, stemming from our fear that we will have to be more than we are to avoid some bad end. So we covet, we envy, we swell up with pride and reach out in gluttony. If there is any lesson grace teaches which is at once difficult and blessed to learn, it is that we do not have to be more than we are. If we trust the creation, even death is not unacceptable; and to tear the fabric of our relationships and self to attempt denying it impoverishes us.

The irony and tragedy of finitude is that no matter how hard we fight against it, we will not win. Even Shakespeare will someday be forgotten. But every act we perform for the purpose of standing against finitude (rather than for its own intrinsic pleasure) diminishes the joy that can be had in living. That joy knows that somebody else eventually will know more, write better, play with more skill; it takes its satisfaction from contributing to the stream of creativity that enriches us all in every age. I am enough, I am even good, but there is or will be someone whose gifts will outstrip mine and I will be forgotten. And thus it should be. But what I have been will remain a part of all who follow.

An especially freeing piece of the acceptance of finitude, and of the dance of grace-filled life, is not knowing what to do next. In all successful therapy there are many moments when the client comes to a new place and confesses that he or she doesn't know what to do. None of the old patterns, plans, and habits work anymore. The client knows that, but the new has not yet been revealed. I usually ask, "Do you have to know what to do, to do something?" The answer is usually no, eventually, because in a truly new situation there is no way to know exactly what to do, and no need to either. What is needed is the courage and the playfulness to do something, confident that if it doesn't work, you can try something else, and something else, and something else, until you get it right. Only the fear of terrible outcomes makes it necessary to be right every time, and the only way to be right every time is to never do anything new. If we lived like that, we would never learn to walk; but as adults we do sometimes believe that we are supposed to appear to know everything. That is an intolerable burden. It imposes a fear and stiffness lest somebody find out that the universal truth is true about us, too: that we sometimes begin actions without knowing where they will end, sometimes guess wrong, and never know all we need to know. What grace teaches us is that sometimes the most beautiful road isn't on the map and we may not know where it comes out. The joy is in the trip, not in being certain of the destination. If the creation and its author are to be trusted, almost any destination is acceptable.

Don't take that as an invitation to be passive, to begin without having a target in mind, but rather as an urging to start out for your target even though you know there is no certainty you will get there. You may get there, and if so, praise the Lord; but if not, you will likely be far better off than if you had sat immobile until perfect certainty came to you.

## EQUALITY AND INTERDEPENDENCE

Much of the grandeur of the Christian victory over sin is in the immense though humble dignity it grants every individual. The Gospels are full of stories in which Jesus made it plain that no one was too insignificant to become the center of his attention or of God's attention, and no one was so great as to have the right to compel it or steal it away from "one of these little ones."

Harry Stack Sullivan had a similar message in his one-genus hypothesis: "We are all simply more alike than different."

In the life of grace no one of us has more right to be considered, more stature, more wholly-owned dominance, than any other. Nor has anyone any less. Such distinctions as emerge among us are temporary and based upon what we actually do to earn them; and that earning is always partial, always influenced by gifts that came to us without our meriting them, and never entitles us to being considered more or less entitled than the next person.

Outside of the sins of pride or envy, our dignity is not compromised when we sit at the table with the thief; nor when we grow too old to work; nor when we are too poor for elegance. Nor do we gain the right to avoid those situations by even the most noble accomplishments. We are free from having to prove ourselves better women, men, or children than the person next door or back home. There is no such thing as a definitely and permanently better or worse person. The Christian message is very clear, and so is our internal message: All have sinned, and God's judgment is upon everyone, as is his grace. No person properly is outside our concern, nor are we outside anyone else's.

The burden of maintaining our proper place, our image, the family name, or what have you, is a false and needless burden if it demands more than making the contribution that is fairly ours to make with the resources we have now. Only our sinfulness demands that we do it as well as our parents did, or as well as we did last year. Our freedom in grace may permit us to do it that well, or better, but it also may give us guidance to try a totally different task or to do the same one in a new way.

The importance of equality in Christian life highlights another crucial theme: the gracious use of power. Power is not a bad thing, neither is it avoidable. When we have it, we can get things done, and some things need doing. Power does get to be a problem when some persons or groups have more than they can use for the good of all. It is inevitable that some people will have more power than others, because they have developed the ability to get more done. For the most part that is good, for it enables people with expertise to use it for the whole society. But sometimes power becomes an end in itself, typically under the control of one of the deadly seven. Somebody stops wanting it for its usefulness and the enjoyment of that usefulness, and instead holds to it as a mark of personal identity, a birthright or a prize to be claimed forever. Then maintaining it becomes the same idolatrous dead end that was described in the previous chapter.

But when a person has more expertise in a given area than others have, power is necessary if he or she is to use it. To waste Abraham Lincoln in a one-room school for forty years wouldn't have helped society. That wasting happens most often when a person with excellent skills has failed for some reason, usually sloth or corporate oppression, to learn how to get power to put those skills to work. Unfortunately, much of our world has been set up so that some groups are systematically prevented from learning how to become powerful; other groups find it to their advantage to maintain the powerlessness. That is a grievous sin, either the corporate sin of building a system that keeps some groups (especially women and racial minorities) powerless, or the personal sin of failure to use opportunities to develop the skills one needs to be effective.

In Christian life each of us is free to develop the power appropriate to our skills and needed to support our other contributions. God wants us to be able to seek the objectives he has helped us identify, and we have the right to learn how to do it. Furthermore, it is enjoyable for grace-filled people to experience the power of others. Persons who have conquered their own pride and envy are free to enjoy and utilize and respond to the power of the other, rather than needing to find ways to undermine and cripple it. Living with powerful people is fun and productive when one knows one's own power and trusts it. It is a gift of Christian life that we sense the pleasure in our own power and that of the persons around us.

When people know their own power and sense their basic equality with one another, despite the many areas in which they are unequal, they also become comfortable with their own individuality. That is perhaps the basic human developmental achievement, to know that one is and has a right to be a separate individual, that one has the power and skill to function outside of any one family or relationship. This is a terribly complicated development that emerges only gradually through the generations of a family's life, but when sloth is conquered it always takes a leap forward. To the extent that our individuation is accomplished, we are free to know ourselves, respond to our bodies and environments, develop commitments, and seek for goals.

The central goal to be achieved, basic to anything else we do with our individuality, our equality, and our power, is the establishment and maintenance of communities. We are all born into a community with at least two members, ourselves and our mothers; and most of us are effectively surrounded at that point in life by effective ties with thousands or even millions—members of our extended family, citizens of a town or city, sharers in the same religion—and by many other connections. Our individuation is the development of the certainty that we have the right to be, even if we move from any or all of these communities and their beliefs and standards. We must know in ourselves the right to choose our community memberships and the way we will relate to them.

But once that right to choose is won, it must be used to reinvest communities—usually the same ones we were first part of, plus some; though in the typical growing up, some of the old ones are relinquished. But it is community, that new (or old) body we elect to join that defines role and identity and status and gives us a place to make our contribution. We measure our well-being according to how well we are connected to our communities and the extent to which we share their goals. We need them—families, companies, churches, nations—to be happy and effective. Without firm ties to communities that endorse us we cannot even be safe, for those who are organized together have vastly more resources at their disposal than does the solitary individual.

We must have our community bonds, but they must be freely chosen or we will be more slaves than partners. And we must work to keep them flexible, because as they grow they get more and more difficult to change when they need changing. But without change when needed, those bonds lose the ability to satisfy and thereby to win the loyalty of people who are committed to abundant life, and more and more the people who are part of them feel less free and fulfilled and more bound and limited.

In a gracious community there is a strong awareness of loyalty, and of the community's need to be something for its members that will win their loyalty freely. There is full

awareness that it is serious business to leave such a union
—be it a nation or a marriage—but if circumstances have
changed and it no longer satisfies or offers hope of satisfying in the future, the separation comes without vengeance.
But such a community knows it is weakened when it loses
a member with whom reconciliation is possible, and it
makes very serious attempts to find out what is troubling
that person and to assess whether his or her needs can be
met by some change in the group. Expression of grievances
is considered an act of love in a group held together by
grace, for it gives others a chance to meet the unmet need
and keep the situation good for all.

Though loyalty to the central mission of the group is vital
in such a body (one is free to reject it by leaving, of course),
in all other ways it is very careful of the freedom of its
members from its own natural tendency to dictate too much
of their lives. It will fight for their liberty to respond to God
and the world in their own way—that is why it comes into
existence. It senses that its goal is the fulfillment of the lives
of its members, that if it cannot achieve this, it has no reason
for being.

Independence and membership in such a community go
hand in hand, for the power of the group is utilized to
preserve its members' freedom, even from each other.
Members of such communions also share a unique relationship with God, as they are invited into the role of co-crea-
tors of the ongoing future of the world. (Isolated individuals are not banned from this possibility in principle, but
their strength is most often sapped by the struggle to survive and the absence of nurturance from others.) All of us
are invited by God to the task of shaping the world for those
who come after us, for developing the skills, the ideas, the
art, the buildings, the morality, and everything else that will
be here for subsequent generations. The most durable
things we create for them are our communions, and probably these are the most important. For it is by membership

in what we have helped those groups become that new generations are shaped into the persons who will carry the hope of humanity into the future.

## ACCEPTABLE AT THE CORE

The most important difference that marks a person freed from slavery to the deadly seven is the certainty that one is acceptable to God and other persons. Though we know we are still vulnerable to sin and will still commit sinful acts, our decisive experience of freedom and forgiveness makes it impossible for us to so despair of the goodness of life that we let life be defined by sin. Life will be defined by hope, which Erikson calls the basic human virtue. Hope is the belief that no matter what the problem is, there is probably a solution; so it is worth the effort to try to find it. It is the certainty that no matter how badly I fail, how embarrassed or guilty I feel, there is still goodness in me that God loves and that is capable of winning the love of persons. It is the vision that the future is always open, that my sins are always forgivable and my inadequacies always remediable through the grace of the God who proclaims, "Behold, I make all things new!"

When I know that what I am is affirmed by the central thrust of all creation, and has been united in love with those who share my communities, then I no longer need to fear sin. I need to be alert to sin in myself and in others, lest they not overpower me nor I betray, but my life does not need to be dominated by the effort to keep away from it. Instead I can devote my life to the love of God and the pouring of myself into the communities that matter to me, making whatever contribution I can to their wholeness, creativity, and power to survive.

In that stance my energy belongs to me, my people, and my God, and it is not bound up in the evil-dominated stance that futilely attempts to defeat sin by inhibition and avoidance. In that expansiveness I am free to dance, to move gracefully and full of hope to those points in the world where humanity can be strengthened and celebrated, or firmly and powerfully to those points where external evil needs to be repelled. As this investment of love in our communities makes them richer, life for their members grows more and more rewarding, and the power of sin to tempt and destroy will be outmatched by the lure of the divine good.

# Notes

1. Morton W. Bloomfield, *The Seven Deadly Sins* (Michigan State University Press, 1952), pp. 1–104.
2. William F. May, *A Catalog of Sins* (Holt, Rinehart & Winston, 1967), p. 201.
3. Billy Graham, *The Seven Deadly Sins* (Zondervan Publishing House, 1956), p. 95.
4. Percy Bysshe Shelley, "Ozymandias"; *John Keats and Percy Bysshe Shelley: Complete Poetical Works* (Modern Library, 1932), p. 589.
5. Karl A. Olsson, *Seven Sins and Seven Virtues* (Harper & Brothers, 1962), p. 20.